Dear Dave and Claudia, Tia and Tracy,
  You will notice (on back cover) that
Jim and I are writers of some of the
stories in this book. We hope you
will enjoy reading about our work
during 40 yrs. in Brazil with the
Ev. Lutheran Ch. in Brazil.
  Much love, Mary and Jim

1998

# SEED FALLING
## On Good Soil

D1318814

Stories From Brazil To Inspire Faith And Commitment

# SEED FALLING
## On Good Soil

Otto C. Tollefson, Editor

With An Historical Perspective By Morris A. Sorenson Jr.

Foreword by James A. Berquist

WINEPRESS **WP** PUBLISHING

ISBN 1-57921-091-0
Library of Congress Catalog Card Number: 97-62571

# In Memoriam

Chris Cheney
Eugene Foehringer
Gaylord Oscar Grant
Gloria Grant
Ruth Nelson
Gary Dean Peterson
Viola Reed
Odin Kenneth Stenberg
Carola Mosby Stenberg
Hubert Willrich

Then I heard a voice from heaven saying,
"Write this: Happy are those who from now on
die in the service of the Lord!"
"Yes indeed!" answers the Spirit.
"They will enjoy rest from their hard work,
because the results of their service go with them."
(Revelation 14:13 TEV)

*"Once there was a man who went out to sow grain . . .*
*But some seeds fell in good soil,*
   *and the plants bore grain:*
      *some had one hundred grains,*
         *others sixty,*
            *and others thirty. . . .*
*And the seeds sown in the good soil stand for those*
   *who hear the message and understand it:*
      *they bear fruit,*
         *some as much as one hundred,*
    *others sixty, and others thirty."*
Matthew 13:3, 8, 23 TEV

# Contents

Foreword   *Dr. James A. Bergquist* . . . . . . . . . . . . . . . . . . . . . . . . . . . xi
Preface   *Otto C. Tollefson* . . . . . . . . . . . . . . . . . . . . . . . . . . . . . . . xv
Introduction   *Dr. Morris A. Sorenson Jr.* . . . . . . . . . . . . . . . . . . . . . xix
Maps . . . . . . . . . . . . . . . . . . . . . . . . . . . . . . . . . . . . . . xxiv, xxv

## PART ONE: THEY HEAR THE WORD AND ACCEPT IT

The Thief Came to Kill   *Otto C. Tollefson* . . . . . . . . . . . . . . . . . . . 29
Ministry at Our Doorstep   *Gary D. Peterson* . . . . . . . . . . . . . . . . . 34
The Light Dawned for Lori   *Elden O. Landvik* . . . . . . . . . . . . . . . 38
God Puts People in Our Path   *Peter E. Mathiasen* . . . . . . . . . . . . . 39
Sent to Reap What Others Had Sown   *John H. Abel* . . . . . . . . . . . 43
The Walls Came a Tumblin' Down   *Elden O. Landvik* . . . . . . . . . . 46
Roadblocks to Ministry   *Andrew Olsen* . . . . . . . . . . . . . . . . . . . . . 47
The Rest of the Flip Chart Story   *Otto C. Tollefson* . . . . . . . . . . . . 49
An Investment That Paid Off   *Jack Aamot* . . . . . . . . . . . . . . . . . . . 52
A Window of Opportunity   *Andrew Olsen* . . . . . . . . . . . . . . . . . . . 56
The Bottom Line   *George Knapp* . . . . . . . . . . . . . . . . . . . . . . . . . . 58
The Long Road to Faith   *Otto C. Tollefson* . . . . . . . . . . . . . . . . . . 60
A Life Changed   *Jack Aamot* . . . . . . . . . . . . . . . . . . . . . . . . . . . . . 64
Saved by the Cross   *Janel Hetland* . . . . . . . . . . . . . . . . . . . . . . . . 66
What Must We Do to Be Saved?   *Viola Reed* . . . . . . . . . . . . . . . . . 68
Margarida's Nunc Dimittis   *Clifford Biel* . . . . . . . . . . . . . . . . . . . . 70

## PART TWO: THEY BEAR FRUIT

Kidnapped—and the Pastor Drove the Getaway Car
  Louis O. Becker . . . . . . . . . . . . . . . . . . . . . . . . . . . . . . . . . 75
The Prayer of Faith Will Save the Sick Man
  Odin Kenneth Stenberg . . . . . . . . . . . . . . . . . . . . . . . . . . . . 80
God's Perfect Timing  Otto C. Tollefson . . . . . . . . . . . . . . . . . . . 83
Christmas in a New Land  Mary Jo Peterson . . . . . . . . . . . . . . . 86
A Heavenly Chorus  Viola Reed . . . . . . . . . . . . . . . . . . . . . . . . 88
More Than a Seasonal Peace  Ann Maland . . . . . . . . . . . . . . . . 89
A Poet Waiting to Get Out  Peter E. Mathiasen . . . . . . . . . . . . . 91
Me, Myself  Maria Edite Lederer . . . . . . . . . . . . . . . . . . . . . . . 94
They Forgave the Murderer  Otto C. Tollefson . . . . . . . . . . . . . . 96
She Didn't Want to Make That Kind of Money
  James L. Peterson . . . . . . . . . . . . . . . . . . . . . . . . . . . . . . . . 98
Still Alive to Tell His Story  Robert H. Fedde . . . . . . . . . . . . . . . 100
Signs of Maturity  Ann Maland . . . . . . . . . . . . . . . . . . . . . . . . 102
Winning the Battle Over the Bottle  James L. Peterson . . . . . . . . 105
Are We Downhearted?  Mary Jo Peterson . . . . . . . . . . . . . . . . 107
Father Is Dying! Can You Come?  Robert H. Fedde . . . . . . . . . . 109
A Rainstorm  Mary Jo Peterson . . . . . . . . . . . . . . . . . . . . . . . 111
Surprised by Forgiveness  Otto C. Tollefson . . . . . . . . . . . . . . . 113
Raulino's Lucky Day  Otto C. Tollefson . . . . . . . . . . . . . . . . . . . 117
Return to the Asphalt Jungle  Robert H. Fedde . . . . . . . . . . . . . 120
God Walked with Them  Otto C. Tollefson . . . . . . . . . . . . . . . . . 122
Freed from Terror  Ruth Kasperson . . . . . . . . . . . . . . . . . . . . . 126
A Norwegian Angel Said, "Fear Not"  Barbara J. Tollefson . . . . . . 128
Doní, Our Brazilian Daughter  Ray Holter . . . . . . . . . . . . . . . . . 130
Jesus Gave Him Peace  Robert Roiko . . . . . . . . . . . . . . . . . . . . 132

## PART THREE: GOD LOVES THE ONE WHO GIVES GLADLY

In the Community of Suffering  Otto C. Tollefson . . . . . . . . . . . . 137
Choking Out Stewardship  Robert H. Fedde . . . . . . . . . . . . . . . 139
Guinea Pigs and Collectors, Steaks and Beer
  Elden O. Landvik . . . . . . . . . . . . . . . . . . . . . . . . . . . . . . . . 141

A New Temple Is Built  *Fayette Massingill* . . . . . . . . . . . . . . . . . . . 143
God Provides  *Charles D. Eidum* . . . . . . . . . . . . . . . . . . . . . . . . . . . 145
The Grace of Giving  *Ruth Holter* . . . . . . . . . . . . . . . . . . . . . . . . . 147
The Man Called Peter  *Robert Maland* . . . . . . . . . . . . . . . . . . . . . 149
A Lady of Culture and Compassion  *Robert Maland* . . . . . . . . . . . 153

## PART FOUR: FAITH ACTIVE IN LOVE

The High Cost of Poverty  *Andrew Olsen* . . . . . . . . . . . . . . . . . . . . . . 157
The One Needle  *Charles D. Eidum* . . . . . . . . . . . . . . . . . . . . . . . . . 159
What Should We Do with All These Beans?  *Ron Baesler* . . . . . . . 161
Whatever Happened to Carlos?  *M. Lorraine Foehringer* . . . . . . . . . 163
What Do You Mean, We're Not Doing Social Work?
    *Odin Kenneth Stenberg* . . . . . . . . . . . . . . . . . . . . . . . . . . . . . . . . . 166
A Field Day for Skeptics  *Don Nelson* . . . . . . . . . . . . . . . . . . . . . . . 171
Now They've Killed the Rich Man's Cow  *Ron Baesler* . . . . . . . . . . 175
Fridolino's Mission  *Charles D. Eidum* . . . . . . . . . . . . . . . . . . . . . . 179
The Philippian Connection  *Richard Wangen* . . . . . . . . . . . . . . . . . 181
Loops, Buffers, Pills, and Shots  *Andrew Olsen* . . . . . . . . . . . . . . . . 185
Grandpa Gene Had a Dream  *M. Lorraine Foehringer* . . . . . . . . . . . 187

Contributors . . . . . . . . . . . . . . . . . . . . . . . . . . . . . . . . . . . . . . . . . . 193

# Foreword

In this book you will encounter sixty stories—plus shorter incidents and remembrances—of mission in Brazil by thirty present and former Lutheran missionaries from North America. Be prepared to be inspired, instructed, and indeed invited into your own missionary journey.

Here are firsthand accounts by long-term, residential missionaries who learned the language and lived among the people they served. Their stories have an authenticity gained by personal experience in primary evangelism and service. Together their reports are told with humor, often with self-deprecation, with a focus on the power of God, not human achievement, and with an evident love for the people and the tasks at hand. These stories take place within Brazilian slums and cities, in remote villages, on untamed frontiers, and wherever faithfulness to the gospel took these servants of Christ. Jesus' parable of Mark 4—and Matthew 13 and Luke 8—is an apt framework for these accounts of the seed, sowers, and soils.

Perhaps a quick glance at the Brazilian context would be helpful in appreciating what is told. Already by 1494, South America was divided by papal decree between the two dominant powers of the period, Portugal and Spain. What is now the nation of Brazil fell to Portugal, an area encompassing about half of the continent. As in the Spanish colonies, in Brazil there was both a history of

imperial cruelty and intense evangelization among the native Indian and the later African slave population by the Roman Catholic
colonizers. When Brazil became independent of Portugal in 1822,
the overwhelming majority of its population were at least nominal
Catholic Christians.

The earliest Lutherans in Brazil were German immigrants, who
began to arrive from 1824 onwards. They were long served by pastors from Germany, or by local pastors trained in a German-lan-
guage seminary in Brazil. By the end of the nineteenth century
other Protestant groups had begun mission in Brazil, with growth
especially notable among various Pentecostal groups.

By 1964 Brazil had fallen under the rule of authoritarian military governments. This period lasted with force until 1985, accompanied by great social inequality, poverty, resistance to the land
reform, and high inflation. By the late 1960s, following Vatican II,
Roman Catholic liberation theology and the base church movement had begun to emerge, facts which began to change the face
of both the Roman Catholic and Protestant churches of Brazil.

The missionaries who have contributed to this book entered
this scene in the 1950s, the 1960s, and later. All were North American. Although an agreement had been reached with the 800,000-
member Evangelical Church of the Lutheran Confession in Brazil
(IECLB), there was some initial uneasiness between the two groups.
The North American Lutherans viewed their mission as one of
evangelical outreach to the whole population of Brazil, not a mission primarily among German ethnics—a position indeed subsequently embraced by the IECLB. The Lutherans of Brazil, too, became truly rooted and contextualized churches within the country. And so in partnership with the host church, and as pastors and
workers of the IECLB, the work of the North American missionaries proceeded.

As these stories tell, the seed bore fruit.

DR. JAMES A. BERGQUIST
President, Lutheran Bible Institute of Seattle

[Editor's note: In 1956, James Bergquist was one of seven students at Luther Theological Seminary, St. Paul, MN, who did joint research on Brazil for a mission class assignment, under Dr. Andrew Burgess. Convinced that Brazil was a field awaiting harvest, they requested the Evangelical Lutheran Church to open mission work in Brazil. Upon ordination in 1958, three of the students, Jack Aamot, Louis Becker, and Peter Mathiasen, were among the first group of missionaries sent to Brazil. James Bergquist went to India.]

# Preface

Come celebrate with us four decades of mission and ministry in Brazil by personnel of the Evangelical Lutheran Church in America (ELCA), the Evangelical Lutheran Church in Canada (ELCC), and their predecessor bodies, in partnership with the Evangelical Church of the Lutheran Confession in Brazil (IECLB). As you read these accounts, join us in thanksgiving to God for the privilege of being among those who were called to sow the Word of God.

This book is divided into four sections: In the first, the stories focus on those who heard the Word and accepted it; in the second, the bearing of fruit in lives of individuals and congregations; in the third, the stewardship of resources; and in the fourth, faith persistently active in love. A number of anecdotes are scattered throughout, capturing some of the lighter moments of living in Brazil.

The contributors, their spouses, places of service in Brazil, and sponsoring congregations are listed at the end of the book. I thank them for their collaboration and trust that my editing enhanced, rather than distorted, their stories. Special thanks to my wife, Barbara—a true partner in mission—for her encouragement and loving patience during this writing and editing process. Our son, Scott, has been my prime motivator, best critic and wisest counselor.

Some stories in this volume are dramatic, others are ordinary, but all give witness to God's faithfulness. We know that we were not alone in people's faith development. We joined hearts and hands with Brazilian, German, and Japanese personnel.

This is not a history of the ELCA's and ELCC's work in Brazil. But some stories necessarily are told in a more detailed historical setting and development.

Dr. Morris A. Sorenson, Jr., has kindly allowed us to include "The Awaiting Soil: An Historical Perspective." This traces the beginnings of our mission and its moving from independence to partnership with the IECLB. I would encourage you to read that first.

Separately, colleague Robert Maland has collected documents, such as correspondence and minutes, that are available from him to those who would wish to pursue that approach. I leave the writing of history to others.

Motivation for this book has come from many sources, not least our last extended visit to Brazil in early 1996. Barbara and I met many pastors and lay persons who spoke of the influence of our ELCA and ELCC personnel in their lives.

One pastor, who we were meeting for the first time, told how Ruth Holter had taken him aside when he was a timid, backward teenager, and said, "You know, Arry, you are a very special person to God."

"And that," the pastor said, "made a decisive difference in my life."

Hearing many such stories, I wanted to share some with our families, sponsoring congregations, and churchwide bodies to tell them that our mutual efforts, by the grace of God, were worth it.

Our ELCA's missionary force in Brazil is now reduced to three couples. This perhaps indicates the effectiveness of our partnership with the IECLB, which now produces a large cadre of pastors, professors, and catechists.

The setting of our mission and ministry varied from old, established areas—industrial, commercial, and agricultural centers—to the new wild west frontier. We served in some of the newest, smallest parishes with no Lutheran background; and in the largest and oldest congregations founded by German Lutheran immigrants.

In some areas the Brazilians were mainly of Portuguese background, mixed with African and native Brazilian blood. In other areas, the people of Germanic ancestry predominated. German was often the language of their home, church, and commerce. In some areas, recent immigrants from Japan formed a large minority.

You will notice that the form of personal address will vary. For the more Luzo-Brazilian, we use *Senhor* for the adult male, and *Senhora* or *Dona* for the adult female. The title is used with the first name as formal address; we often did not know or have forgotten family names. Among the people of German ancestry, we typically used *Herr* and *Frau* with the last name. For example, a woman may be known both as *Frau* Zeiler and *Dona* Traudy. In some stories, the names of Brazilians have been changed, out of courtesy. Those changes are noted at the end of the stories.

Come, meet your brothers and sisters in the faith. Join us in seeing how God's Word bore fruit in those who heard and understood. And laugh with us at some of our language and cultural bloopers.

OTTO C. TOLLEFSON

# The Awaiting Soil:
# An Historical Perspective

*Morris A. Sorenson Jr.*

In 1966, the Rev. Morris A. Sorenson Jr. was called by the Board of World Missions of the American Lutheran Church (ALC) to serve as an area secretary on the staff of the division. His specific responsibilities were Brazil, Colombia, Mexico, and New Guinea. He assumed these responsibilities on July 1, 1966, and concluded them on June 30, 1970, when he became director of the division.

During this period, Dr. Sorenson played a vital role in the development of a written agreement with the Evangelical Church of the Lutheran Confession in Brazil (IECLB), defining the nature of the ALC's work in that place. This agreement was valuable to the national church as it attempted to use all of its resources effectively in mission.

During his years as an area secretary, and later as the director of the division, he gave a great deal of time to the development of agreements that were theologically and missiologically sound.

As he began his work with the church and mission in Brazil, he wrote "An Historical Glimpse." The following excerpt from that document summarizes, as well as puts into perspective, the mission of the Lutheran missionaries in Brazil.

The largest non-Pentecostal Protestant church in Latin America is the Evangelical Church of the Lutheran Confession in Brazil, which numbers 703,078 baptized members with a ministerium of 248 (1965 statistics). The IECLB, composed primarily of people of German descent, has a Brazilian history of more than one hundred years.

There is another Lutheran Church in Brazil, related to the Lutheran Church-Missouri Synod (LCMS), which numbers over one hundred thousand members who are also largely of German descent. For exceedingly complex historical reasons, the relationship between these churches has never been vital.

The Evangelical Lutheran Church (ELC) began work in Brazil in 1958, in keeping with a resolution of the 1956 General Convention of the Church. In beginning work, the ELC assumed that which had been begun in the northwestern section of the state of Paraná by the World Mission Prayer League, as of its entrance into Brazil in 1954. The beginning of work by the ELC was accompanied, unfortunately, by considerable misunderstanding and tension with the IECLB. These misunderstandings and tensions centered, I believe, in three things:

1. The circumstances that accompanied the entrance of the LCMS missionaries into Brazil early in the century and the ensuing formation of a separate church, created a long-lasting suspicion within the IECLB of North American Lutheran mission activity.
2. The apparent necessity of a North American Lutheran church beginning work in Brazil caused the IECLB to admit, though not openly, that evangelism and new work was something that they themselves should have undertaken long before missionaries of our church appeared on the scene.
3. The IECLB, after a long and difficult struggle to establish itself in a Roman Catholic nation, had resolved the problem of relationship with both the Roman Catholic Church and the state by limiting itself to a ministry directed to ethnic Germans. The church was not, therefore, proselytizing among the Roman Catholics and was

concerned primarily with "keeping their own house in order." The appearance of aggressive North American Lutherans endangered, at least in their thinking, the sensitive balance that had been established in Roman Catholic Brazil.

For these reasons the IECLB actively protested the establishment of ELC work in Brazil.

Nevertheless, missionaries of the ELC began work in Brazil. The first missionaries . . . were assigned to northwestern Paraná and several cities in the western part of São Paulo. This work, much of it still being carried on by missionaries of the ALC, was, for the most part, pioneer evangelism in "frontier" communities. Out of these early beginnings, small Christian churches have developed in most of the communities in which work was begun.

By 1962, misunderstandings and tensions between the IECLB and the ALC had been largely dispelled. In fact, by then, on request of the church, several missionaries of the ALC were assigned to parishes of the IECLB. A relationship of understanding and harmony continued to develop between the groups, and in 1964 an agreement was negotiated between the church and mission.

A maturing relationship and growth in mutual respect led to the writing of a revised agreement, dated December 8, 1969. This agreement was a significant milestone in relationships. The spirit and general direction of the relationship, as delineated in the agreement, served Lutheran ministry well in Brazil.

As the area secretary for Brazil, Dr. Sorenson made three extended visits there in 1967, 1968, and 1969. His agenda in Brazil was rather straightforward:

1. *To further develop and implement the agreement of the ALC with the IECLB.*

The 1969 agreement was illustrative of most agreements reached in several areas of the world. The matters of personnel assignments, calls, salaries, and participation in the IECLB were given serious consideration and were reflected in the agreement.

2. *To assist the missionary community in the consideration of how best to meet the educational needs of their children.*

   When I arrived in Brazil for my first visit, I did so with a mandate from the division director, Dr. T. P. Fricke, to understand the educational needs of the missionary community and to assist them in shaping a meaningful response to these needs. In 1966, the Brazil mission was conducting an educational program for its primary school children in Londrina. Some children, including high school students, were studying in a private school in São Paulo. Other children were studying in The American School in Campinas, and some in Brazilian schools in the communities where their parents lived and worked. In addition thereto, some favored a more generous use of Augustana Academy in Canton, South Dakota. At the January 1967 conference, the mission voted to close the school in Londrina and establish a hostel in Campinas near The American School. The Londrina school was to be closed in June 1968, and the new hostel was to be ready for occupancy in the fall that year. This I believed to be a happy solution to a difficult problem. The Lord was clearly at work with the conference when this decision was made. Concurrently with the opening of the hostel in Campinas, Donald and Lillian Aarsvold, laypersons from Kasson, Minnesota, were called as houseparents. Their contribution was superb. They were the right persons for this new responsibility.

3. *To provide personal help and pastoral care for the missionary community.*

   Though there was a measure of success in the fulfillment of this agenda item, I was disappointed in the rather large exit of capable young missionaries from Brazil. How I wished they would have stayed a longer period!

The missionaries who served in Brazil during this period had the opportunity for a most exciting ministry. In a way, almost unknown to early missionaries, they were privileged to speak to the church as they spoke to the world. God granted them the joy of being both an instrument in and a witness to a significant renewal in the church. At the same time, out of a context of a renewed Christian fellowship, they had almost unlimited opportunity and freedom to present Christ to those who were not yet a part of the communion of saints. The challenge in Brazil was great. Opportunities were almost unlimited, and the joy in which the missionaries ministered was a cause for great thanksgiving.*

---

\* Edited from *Beyond Expectation* by Morris A. Sorenson Jr. and Dorothy A. Sorenson. Copyright 1996. Used by permission.

# Central and Southern Brazil

# Part One

## They Hear the Word and Accept It

# The Thief Came to Kill

*Otto C. Tollefson*

Salette, I'll give you bread and water! Salette, I'll give you bread and water." A demonic voice repeatedly screamed out its counteroffer to Salette as I read the promises of Jesus.

It happened in Umuarama, Paraná, a small frontier town. I was conducting a two week evening Bible course in the Lutheran church, together with Jim Petersen, now one of the international directors of the Navigators. We were guests of missionary pastor Jim Hougen and his wife, Miriam.

On Monday noon, as we sat down for dinner, some Presbyterian Christians asked if we could help them since their pastors had left on an extended trip earlier that morning.

They believed Salette, a sixteen-year-old girl, had been possessed by a demon the night before. We listened attentively as they recounted how that Sunday evening she had attended their church. The pastor had given an invitation to those who wanted to accept Jesus as their Lord and Savior to come forward for prayer. Salette had stood up, left the back bench where she had been seated, and began walking down the aisle with others.

Some in the congregation had audibly gasped as Salette suddenly began walking backward to the bench where she had been seated. It was as though she were being pulled back by a strong, unseen force.

In the morning the word quickly spread that Salette was possessed by an evil spirit. A medical doctor had confirmed it. The family then called for the *benzedeira* (witch doctor, sorceress) from the local spiritualist center. She had visited the girl, performed rituals, and tied blue ribbons on her. It was to no avail; Salette continued under the power of the demon.

The family then agreed to call for the Presbyterian pastors. As luck—or providence—would have it, they were out of town. The Presbyterians sought out Pastor Hougen.

After discussing this over dinner, we three men, who had heard only vague stories of evil spirits and exorcisms, prayed with a good dose of fear and uneasiness. We asked specifically for three things: discernment to what was happening, wisdom to know what to do and say, and God's protection against the trickery of the evil one.

As the two Jims and I entered the living room of the simple wooden house, we saw Salette sitting on a daybed. Family, neighbors, and Presbyterian church members crowded the room. The demon, speaking through Salette, immediately snarled at us and ridiculed all believers in Christ.

I was surprised when the voice laughed at us three, one by one, with specific, sarcastic comments that individually fit us. To me, "You, with those glasses! What do you wear them for?" It knew of my self-consciousness about wearing glasses! My offer to remove them brought only more ridicule. Without comparing notes, we discerned that this was of the evil one.

Now for wisdom in what to do. I felt relieved when Jim Petersen approached Salette, sat on the couch at her feet, and began talking. Jim Hougen and I prayed silently. After a few minutes Jim Petersen turned to me and, without warning, said, "Otto, you take over."

Not knowing what else to do, I also sat on the couch next to Salette and opened my Bible. The demon in Salette continued laughing and sneering, ranting and raving. I ignored it as I directed my words in clear, strong tones to Salette, hoping that she would hear.

"Salette," I said, "I want to read to you God's Word." I began reading from the tenth chapter of John's Gospel.

As I read, there was ongoing laughter and sneering from the demon speaking through Salette. But when I read Jesus' words, "I am the gate. Whoever enters by me will be saved; and will come in and go out and find pasture," the demon began screaming repeatedly, "Salette, I'll give you bread and water. Salette, I'll give you bread and water."

I stopped for a few moments, but the demon continued loudly, nonstop, in machine-gun fashion, "Salette, I'll give you bread and water." I perceived that the demon was jamming communication so Salette would not hear the promise of Jesus, even in her subconscious.

I continued with the tenth verse, "The thief comes only in order to steal and kill and destroy." A piercing, bloodcurdling screech came from Salette's mouth when I said the word *kill*. I repeated the sentence a few more times, and the same screech came on the word kill. I had hit the vulnerable nerve in this demon.

The demon then changed tactics and began to sneer at me for being a believer. I may not have consciously remembered that I wore the helmet of salvation and the breastplate of Christ's righteousness. Instead of directing my words to Salette, I began for the first time to confront the demon with the affirmation, "Through Jesus *I* am holy. *You* are the murderer. *I* am holy. *You* are the murderer. *You* have come only to steal and kill and destroy. *Jesus* has come to give Salette life in all its fullness."

I persisted in my confession of who I was in Christ and in my accusation of the demon. Eventually the demon grew quiet and confessed, "I didn't want to do it. I was sent." In Jesus' name I commanded it to return to the place from where it had come. But it pleaded in an agonizing wail to allow it to return to the jungle that bordered the town. I did not accept such negotiation.

The story is much longer. But the ending is that the demon left Salette at my insistent commands in the name of Jesus. Salette's exhausted body finally relaxed in sleep.

On our return to the Hougen home, the two Jims asked if I had experienced any fear of bodily harm. "Of course not," was my surprised reply. "Should I have?"

Jim Petersen explained, "Weren't you aware that the demon was desperately trying to slap and hit you, to knee you in the groin—and never once could touch you? It always stopped short!" I had not been aware of it. God had given me mental concentration and physical protection.

Later we learned that within a few hours after we had left Salette's home, her parents again allowed the *benzedeira* (sorceress) to enter the room. Immediately the demon had returned to take possession of Salette. She was taken to a spiritualist center; their medium failed to exorcise the evil spirit. Five days later it suddenly departed. Salette was extremely tired but back to normal. We agreed with the Presbyterians that as long as the family allowed the *benzedeira* and spiritualist center to be involved, our efforts would be undermined.

A week later I stopped by Salette's home to pick up my umbrella, which I had left there. I asked permission to speak with her. I questioned her if she knew me, if she had ever seen or talked with me or recognized my voice. To all of my questions, she answered no. It confirmed our conviction that we had had an encounter with an evil spirit who had entered her body. We believe that during this encounter we never spoke with Salette but only with the evil spirit.

We left her in the care of the Presbyterian pastors.

What had I learned? What were the results for my life?

- Portions of Scripture came alive in a new way.
- I gained a greater confidence in the authority and power of the Word of God.
- When we speak "in the name of Jesus," it is as though we have been given power of attorney to act on his behalf.
- There is evil in the world. We do not fight against flesh and blood but against the power of demonic forces.
- Prayer and fasting are essential preparation.
- The Holy Spirit gives gifts to the body of Christ that are needed for ministry. We had received the gifts of discernment and faith.

- The armor of God (the helmet of salvation and the breastplate of righteousness) is for our physical and spiritual protection.
- We use the Word of God when we go on the offensive.
- We don't play around with the occult or the spirit world.
- The demonic seeks to jam the communication line between God and us.
- The demons can call us by name, but Jesus also knows and calls us by name!
- The demonic counteroffers God's promises.

What a privilege we have to announce the clear promise of Jesus, "I am come in order that you might have life—life in all its fullness" (John 10:10 TEV). I can only pray that Salette came to accept the life that the demonic thief wanted to steal from her.

### BAD TO THE LAST DROP

Coffee is a vital part of Brazilian life. On the Paraná frontier, pots of it simmered all day on the back burner of a home's wood burning cook stove, ready to be savored in demitasse cups throughout the day.

The new missionaries often struggled to enjoy such coffee before becoming addicted, however.

A friend told of visiting in a home where the woman graciously served him a steaming cup of her strong, syrupy coffee. He found the drink intolerable but did not wish to offend her. When the hostess turned her back, he quickly emptied his cup through the open, unscreened window next to where he was sitting.

Imagine his embarrassment when he heard screams of pain, followed by shouts of "Who threw hot coffee on us?" coming from the woman's children who were playing under the window.

—Ruth Kasperson

# Ministry at Our Doorstep

*Gary D. Peterson*

Four-year-old Marilene was dying. Even our untrained eyes could see this as we entered the hospital room. My wife, Karlene, was seven months pregnant. She knelt on the floor beside the dark-haired mother, Ely. Soon the tears mingled silently on their cheeks. I went to tall, haggard, and unshaven Otílio, who was keeping vigil by his daughter's bed. Pain was etched in his eyes. Karlene and I shared God's love and our hope in Jesus. Our desire was to give strength to this young couple as we shared in their ordeal.

Little did we know that day how God would use our ministry to this family. We had been in the little town of Pedro Osório about eight months and felt discouraged. Sunday attendance at our chapel dropped as Christmas approached. Worry about finances gnawed at my mind. That month inflation had soared to forty-eight percent, sharply cutting our purchasing power.

Then God sent Otílio and Ely to us. One sunny January morning, as we finished breakfast with a prayer that our Lord would use our ministry, someone knocked at the door. We opened it to find a couple dressed in the black clothes of mourning with a look of urgency and worry on their faces. They asked us to drive them and their little daughter to the large hospital in Pelotas where she could receive surgery for a blocked intestine.

Inwardly I was suspicious. Some of our people wanted to use us and our car as a free taxi service, and we had determined that must stop. The urgency in this couple's eyes touched me, however, and we soon picked up a feverish Marilene at the local, one-doctor hospital for the bumpy, dusty, hour long trip to the city.

Marilene's condition and our urgency did not result in immediate attention, however. It turned into a long, anxious day of waiting. About 9:00 P.M. the surgeon showed us the large section of intestine that had been removed. He was confident and encouraging. The worst seemed over, and we felt very close to Otílio and Ely after sharing their burden of anxiety and concern. With a prayer of thanksgiving, Karlene and I went home to rest.

Our confidence was shattered the next morning when we saw Marilene's condition.

No doctor had come; no antibiotics had been given. We were used to TV dramas of doctors and nurses scrambling to save lives, but there was none of this. I felt angry that someone had apparently just decided to let her die. It seemed callous, inhuman, and unfair!

As we lived the ordeal of watching their daughter's life ebb away, Karlene and I could only remind them of God's love and their hope in Jesus, pray with them, and offer them our strength. They expressed surprise that we stayed with them, for it was not the practice of priests or pastors to minister in this personal way with hurting, grieving people.

First we prayed for healing. Finally we surrendered Marilene into the hands of her loving, heavenly Father, asking for an answer soon. After only a few minutes, her face began to turn a waxy yellow; her breathing became more shallow and then stopped. Moans and cries filled the room. Karlene held Ely in her arms; I sobbed along with Otílio. We prayed together and quietly made plans for the funeral the next day. (In Brazil, with no embalming, interment must be completed within twenty-four hours of a death.)

The next day in the tiny village of Alto Alegre, I held the service in a large machinery shed. Through tears I struggled to speak to the two hundred family members and friends of the hope we have in Jesus. I shared God's love for Marilene and for them.

We carried the little casket up the hill to an open grave in the town cemetery. There I reminded the people that death and the grave could not hold Jesus, the Lord of life, nor his people.

This was our first opportunity to minister deeply to our people.

Then our ministry opened up in a new way. We began a Bible study in Alto Alegre with about thirty people gathering for songs, study, and prayer in the back of the general store owned by Otílio's boss. Kerosene lamps lit the room as God's Word, "a lamp unto my feet," spoke to those simple folk. Soon most of them had received Jesus as Savior and Lord.

Next we were invited to hold Bible studies in the home of Ely's family, farther up in the hills. Up there, our Jeep station wagon often got stuck in the mud. One rainy night we all piled out to cut brush to put under the wheels and push. Back at their house, Ely filled a wooden trough and washed Karlene's muddy feet. She was nearly dumbfounded when the pastor's wife knelt in turn to wash her feet! There was to be no class distinction in this friendship.

One night in the *vila*, I explained the way of salvation and invited all who wished to receive Jesus as Savior and Lord to stand up—and all thirteen people, two whole families, stood up!

*Hey, wait a minute!* I thought, *Maybe they didn't understand me correctly.* So I had them all sit down again. They were not, I told them, just joining the church or doing it to please me. They were inviting Jesus into their lives, trusting him alone for salvation, committing themselves to study his Word and learn his ways, to talk with him in prayer and live to please him. Again I invited them to stand if they wanted to receive Jesus. And they all stood up!

Later I cautiously suggested to my district supervising pastor, a German who had been pioneering Lutheran congregations for many years, that what our nominal Lutherans needed was conversion—a conscious, personal commitment to Jesus Christ. He not only agreed but asked me to present a paper on conversion at our pastors' meeting. He also put me in charge of training lay evangelists for our district.

Our congregation at Pedro Osório began planning a citywide evangelism campaign, but God didn't wait. Instead he started one of his own! My "volleyball evangelism" on a court outside our backdoor netted two young men, both school dropouts with no family life, who started Bible studies with me. Soon they accepted Christ and walked around town whistling and singing Christian songs.

In small group Bible studies, in nose-to-nose sharing with individuals, even in altar calls (unusual for Lutherans!), people responded to the gospel. In six weeks, fifty-seven people committed their lives to Jesus Christ, and we hadn't even begun the evangelism campaign!

Our prayer that January morning wasn't the first time we had asked God to use us in ministry. I can't explain why that day God sent someone and opened things up in such a miraculous way. I only know that God does take our prayers seriously, and, if we want to be used, there are people who need the caring and love only we Christians can give. God didn't cause Marilene's blocked intestine or her death, but I'm convinced God did send Otílio and Ely to us. It scares me to think what would not have happened if my suspicions about being manipulated had overwhelmed my sensitivity to these people at our doorstep.

* Edited version of "Ministry at Our Doorstep," first published in *Evangel*, Light and Light Press, January 6, 1985. Used by permission of Karlene Peterson.

# The Light Dawned for Lori

*Elden O. Landvik*

Lori had heard it all before. She was attentive as I taught, but the good news seemed to be for her neither especially good nor new. But one night that was to change.

Lori was one of a handful from our large congregation in Taquara, Rio Grande do Sul, who came regularly to our midweek Bible studies. She was a young mother, upper-middle class, an elementary teacher, who worshiped sporadically. Our theme was God's way of salvation.

In that setting where Lutheranism was often more an inherited culture than a faith relationship, I sensed a need to stress that we can never merit God's great salvation. Nor can we earn it. I tried to find ways to make certain they understood that it must be all of God's grace. Salvation can only be received as a gift, a gift Jesus had purchased for us with his life, death, and resurrection.

Lori had heard all this before. But one night, Lori's face suddenly lit up as she interrupted with an exclamation of sheer excitement, *"É isso mesmo!"* That's exactly it!

The light of the gospel had dawned in her heart. The Holy Spirit had made the spoken word a living, transforming word. It was evident on Lori's face. It was evident in her life during our remaining years in Taquara.

# God Puts People in Our Path

*Peter E. Mathiasen*

There were no Lutherans waiting for my wife, Elna, and me when we arrived in Loanda, Paraná, in October 1959. This interior town being carved out in the jungles of Brazil had been chosen as the site for our mission. In that wild west setting we discovered that casual contacts could have life-changing consequences under God's guidance.

One of the first persons I met was Manolo. I had ruined a tire on the city's main street. Manolo had a tire shop only a few blocks away, and he repaired the tire.

That was all. Nothing more. I remember he was high on *pinga* (a local cheap but strong rum), but that was typical of him, as I was to learn later.

We searched for a storefront to hold services. The club across from Manolo's shop wasn't holding dances during Lent, so we arranged to have a week of evangelistic preaching there.

I was pleased to note that Manolo was among the thirty or forty curious people in attendance the first night. I can't remember anything unusual about the service. Bob Kasperson, the only missionary with a few years of experience, preached. Viola Reed provided musical accompaniment on her accordion.

As I greeted people at the door, Manolo said, "Pastor, if you want to convert me, I'm ready to be converted."

People are rarely that cooperative! I answered, "I can't convert anyone. Only God can do that." A few weeks later we held a vacation Bible school in a one-room schoolhouse. Manolo's three children, Mercedes, Edna, and Edson, were among the fifty children who attended. They and their mother, Natalia, eventually became a part of our first group of members in Loanda, but not Manolo. He wasn't ready yet. Quiet Natalia became the spiritual dynamo in that family. She was a woman of prayer who exercised her quiet influence with the other family members.

Manolo basically had no religion. Although Brazil is generally known as a Roman Catholic country, Manolo's nominal Catholic family had come under the influence of spiritism, the belief that spirits of the dead can communicate with the living.

During this time he was often under the influence of *pinga.* He barely managed to provide for his beautiful family with income from his junkyard and tire repair shop.

Natalia worried when their son, Edson, would come to Sunday school in the morning with his sisters but would skip church on Sunday evenings to go the movies instead.

Edson was in our first confirmation class. On the night before he was to be confirmed, he came to me and said, "Pastor, I'm not ready for confirmation." At first I thought it was the night-before jitters, but it was deeper than that. We talked for more than an hour.

"Edson, I respect your decision," I said. "If you were to be confirmed tomorrow, you wouldn't be able to make your vows with a clear conscience." In that society there was a stigma attached to being known as a *crente,* a believer following a public profession of faith.

A year later Edson was ready to make his vows with conviction, and he courageously affirmed his faith.

Edson moved from Loanda to Joinville, Santa Catarina, so he could go to college. He lived with Pastor Otto and Barbara Tollefson during his three years of study. He supported himself and developed his natural teaching abilities by working half-days for the Lutheran congregation as a religious education instructor in public schools. He endeared himself to the children. He demonstrated his gift as a youth leader and participated actively in pioneering new parish stewardship and evangelism programs.

After college, he faced a formidable challenge when he enrolled in the Lutheran church's theological seminary in São Leopoldo, Rio Grande do Sul. At that time most of the classes were taught in German, and Edson did not speak German. Classmates translated the lectures into Portuguese for him. Although he studied German, he never did master the language. Still he graduated with distinction, becoming the first student from the theological seminary to do so without being able to speak German!

In 1974, Edson took a call to Caxias do Sul, in the heart of Rio Grande do Sul's Italian Catholic community, with a strong contingency of Lutherans of German ancestry. The congregation used Portuguese as its primary language. That year I had the joy of presiding at his marriage to Erica.

The next year my wife and I left Brazil to return to Canada permanently. Twenty years later, in November 1995, I visited Edson and Erica and their three children in Florianópolis, the capital city of Santa Catarina.

Under his leadership the congregation has an extraordinary vision for ministry and mission. It has three youth groups. The one I visited had forty participants between thirteen and sixteen years of age. Besides the morning worship services, there are Sunday evening youth services. Sixteen Bible study groups meet regularly, ten of them for married couples.

The parish has given birth to two congregations, one of which is now large enough to be a separate parish. There are plans to begin a new congregation in another area of the city. A large amount of Edson's time is dedicated to counseling. In addition to serving as a pastor in that large parish, Edson is a part-time evangelist in the Evangelical Church of the Lutheran Confession in Brazil (IECLB).

On the Sunday I attended, the church was packed, as it normally is. Erica directed the youth orchestra; Edson preached. At the conclusion of the service, he presented me to the congregation as the pastor who had first introduced his family to the Scriptures and to Christ.

He told the congregation how his family had been enmeshed in spiritism and how God's Word had set them free. I was deeply moved when he said, "I am convinced that God puts people in our path at the right time in our lives. That was the right time for my family and me."

He recounted how years later his father, Manolo, became a Christian and overcame his problem with alcohol. He shared how his aunts and uncles, one by one, were brought to faith. Last of all was an uncle who had been very wealthy but had lost everything in bankruptcy before God was able to reach him.

I reflected on how there had been no Lutherans waiting for us when we arrived in Loanda. After a decade of missionary evangelism (1959–1968), there are now most likely no Lutherans in Loanda because the congregation disbanded after all members moved away. But God has graciously multiplied the seed that was sown during the ten years of mission and ministry.

Almost forty years have passed since my ruined tire brought about that first meeting with Manolo in the tire repair shop. Casual contacts can have life-giving significance under God's guidance.

---

* This is an edited and expanded version of *Brazilian Encounters*. Copyright by Peter E. Mathiasen. Used by permission.

# Sent to Reap What Others Had Sown

*John H. Abel*

During my first years in Brazil, I experienced how God often works in the lives of people long before the missionary arrives, and then, almost like a divine appointment, the missionary appears on the scene.

This was the case with Francisco and Geni Cavalcanti, our first converts after we arrived in the new frontier town of Cianorte, in northern Paraná. Cianorte had been literally cut out of the jungle in 1953. Our family and our Japanese colleague, Miss Kiyoko Suda, arrived in November 1954. There was not so much as a grade school, but already there were over one hundred houses. People were arriving in this wild west settlement by the dozens every day in search of a better life in a new land. The city government had not yet been organized, but candidates and parties were gearing up for a coming election.

We rented a storefront building in the commercial center. Ruby and I and our three small boys lived in the three rooms connected to this storefront.

The first activity we planned for this building was our Lutheran church, and the second, a school. I had a model of a short bench with a back that could be let down to serve as a writing area. Each bench needed to double as a desk for two students. We planned to open the first grade school in town in February 1955. I ordered fifteen benches at a small furniture shop a couple blocks away.

The shop owner agreed to cut all the lumber and drill the holes and to allow me to assemble and varnish the benches. There I first met Francisco Cavalcanti. When Francisco came to deliver the parts for me to assemble, however, he explained, "I don't know if you'll be able to get them together and rub the varnish on right. I think I should come over after work and help for a couple nights."

It seemed this was the Lord's doing, for it gave me an opportunity to get to know Francisco and his wife, Geni. Many evenings over the next few weeks, we worked until about nine o'clock, and then I took him home in my Jeep. We went into his house and had a short Bible study.

They had been given a Bible by some friends in the city where they lived before moving to Cianorte. Geni's father had been murdered, and the cultural expectation was that Francisco would take revenge on the guilty ones. They relocated two hundred miles away to this new town to avoid getting involved in a bloody feud.

Francisco and Geni were so sincerely interested in the Bible's good news that it was not long before I presented God's plan of salvation, and they received Christ as their Lord and Savior. From then on they came faithfully to all our church services. Within a few months they and their infant daughter were baptized and received as members of our first Lutheran congregation.

In 1958, we were assigned to Londrina but often had occasion to drive to Cianorte where we kept in touch with Francisco, who was then a deacon on the church board.

In 1959, when Otis and Kay Lee came to Londrina to develop a Bible school, Francisco and Geni were among our first students. After a year in Bible school, they followed the western movement to the new town of Umuarama where they became the nucleus of a new Lutheran mission. Francisco led the Sunday school and conducted worship services, alternating Sundays with the missionary pastors from Cianorte.

Previously when they had lived in Cianorte, I had taught Francisco to drive and helped him get his driver's license. He bought a used Jeep and became a taxi driver. Later he went into selling rural real estate. Following the western movement, Francisco and Geni eventually lived on a large farm in Mato Grosso State. When there was no Lutheran congregation in the area, they worked with the Presbyterian church. Their gentle spirit and winsome witnessing were a blessing to many.

An interesting sequel is that in the mid-1980s, their daughter, Zenilda, and her husband attended the new church Ruby and I were beginning in Curitiba.

We had harvested where others unknown to us had planted the seed. It was as Jesus said, "I have sent you to reap a harvest in a field where you did not work; others worked there, and you profit from their work" (John 4:38 TEV). And in God's gracious providence, we were able to see spiritual fruit in our first converts down to the third generation. Indeed, the seed of God's Word had fallen on good soil.

## NAILED BY THE DICTIONARY

Louis Becker, ever the handyman, needed nails for shelves in their home. He consulted his dictionary for nails and wrote down the first word. At the store, instead of requesting *pregos,* carpenter nails, he confidently asked for half a kilo of *unhas,* fingernails.

# The Walls Came a Tumblin' Down

*Elden O. Landvik*

When we arrived to serve the Taquara congregation, we found the church building in a state of utter disrepair. The stucco exterior had been painted many years previously, but the intervening years had worn the paint away, and the church had taken on the dismal color of the red soil that surrounded it.

Even more of a problem to me, however, was the six-foot high brick wall that surrounded the entire church lot. Glass shards had been embedded in the concrete cap on top of the wall. Above these were three rows of barbed wire. I understood they had been installed to keep out thieves. But the message the church was announcing to the public seemed to be, "Stay away. We don't want you here."

With some encouragement the church council decided to paint the building and tear down that threatening wall. Where the wall had been, they created colorful flower beds.

One of my missionary colleagues once said, "Everything we do is evangelism." In a sense, that's true. We wanted the church facility to announce to the community what the Lord of the church says: "Come! You are welcome."

# Roadblocks to Ministry

*Andrew Olsen*

There were no lions to face in Brazil as Daniel of old did in Babylon, but angry and determined truck drivers can be as threatening.

I was on a Good Samaritan mission: Nello Pardini, a member of our church in Paranavaí, needed emergency surgery in Londrina, only 220 kilometers away. The first 70 kilometers would be a well-traveled dirt road that would be passable if the rains held off; the last 150 would be asphalt. The trip usually took about three hours one way.

I needed to get back quickly because Miss Toshiko Arai, our Japanese missionary colleague, and I were starting a one week series of evangelistic meetings the next evening in Paranavaí.

As we hurriedly drove off in the middle of the night, we prayed not only for Nello's health but for our safety and success in facing the lions in our path. Thousands of truck drivers throughout Brazil had called a wildcat strike in response to an attempt by the national government to limit weight on the roads. Trucks piled high with logs, lumber, rice, beans, and fresh fruits lined the roadways.

We were stopped by barricades on entering and leaving a dozen villages and towns. At each point I knew I would have only a few moments to be convincing with a good story. At each point the tough truck drivers appeared antagonistic as they milled around, keeping warm by the piles of burning tires.

My words were simple and direct: we were on a mission of life and death. It may be that they reluctantly allowed us to pass because they knew they had already paralyzed the nation. It took us twelve hours to reach the hospital.

I left Nello at the hospital and started back, again facing the same roadblocks and tough truckers that demanded a convincing story. Once again, I explained it was a matter of life and death—I had pastoral responsibilities waiting for me. God graciously gave the roadblockers understanding hearts.

I arrived in Paranavaí with a half hour to spare, thanking God for closing the mouths of lions on the Paraná highway.

### READ TO LIVE

I have been helping a few women to learn to read. We meet three afternoons a week. Our maid is also studying with me in the evenings. Several of them expressed their desire to read so they would be able to study the Bible. One lady said, "All my life, I've had to listen to what other people say the Bible teaches, but I want to study it for myself so I'll know what to believe."

She knows that she is an unsaved sinner and is very open to the Word and seems to drink in the opening devotions. I am trusting the Lord to do a work of grace in her heart as well as in the others.

—*Ruth Kasperson*, Cianorte, Paraná
In a letter, dated June 9, 1958

# The Rest of the Flip Chart Story

*Otto C. Tollefson*

I was perturbed that the long line was moving so slowly in the scorching afternoon sun. It was coffee break time at the *Encontrão,* Encounter Movement's leadership meeting in Florianópolis, on March 22, 1996. I turned to introduce myself to a man behind me; he was Vili Schneider, a dairy farmer from Cruz Alta, Rio Grande do Sul. When I mentioned that one of our American pastors had served there many years ago, Vili corrected me. "Actually, there had been two," he said, "Ray Holter and David Nelson."

"But they wouldn't know me," he quickly added. "I was outside the church and the faith then. Well, Holter might remember a baptism when I was a sponsor. As soon as the baby was baptized, the whole family walked out, not staying for the rest of the service." Vili explained, "We went home to get the *festa* (celebration party) going."

Vili then told me how he had been converted years later under Walter Ludwig, a Brazilian pastor. When his pastor invited him to be a part of a team to make home evangelism visits, he initially refused. Vili was too scared to do so. But his pastor assured him he could overcome his fear by using one of the three copies of a flip chart the Americans had left in the parish. It was called *O Abismo Ligado,* or The Abyss Connected. It's often referred to as the bridge illustration—how we are reconnected to God by Christ.

I assured Vili I was acquainted with the flip chart. He recounted how he had practiced the narration for each picture: God being holy; people being sinners; our need for reconciliation; how our good works and religiosity are like timbers too short to bridge the gap; but how Christ's death is the bridge through which we come into relationship with God. A door represents Christ waiting for our response to his call and knock, and the open hands symbolize our receiving Jesus through faith.

Before going out with the evangelism team, Vili gathered his two little daughters for a final practice on them. Later that week he made the presentation to his father who was converted through it. "Now gospel finally makes sense!" he had said, excitedly.

With tears in his eyes, Vili recalled that his six-year-old daughter then told him, "Daddy, I also asked Jesus into my life." Surprised, he asked her how and when. "The other night," she replied, "when you practiced telling us the story." He saw the joy and difference in her life. She went on to study sacred music and is now married to a Lutheran pastor.

When Vili was done telling me his story, I asked if he'd like to hear the story of that flip chart from the beginning. I recounted how in 1958, while in language school, I had found some black and white illustrated gospel booklets entitled, *O Abismo Ligado.* About three years later, I had some booklets with me when Pastor Robert Fedde and I were in Umuarama, a new frontier town, for a week of visitation, teaching, and preaching in our little storefront branch church. The first morning we began going door-to-door, leaving a gospel tract with an invitation for the evening sessions.

When Bob saw the *Abismo Ligado* material, he suggested we stop immediately to go buy notebooks with blank sheets. We spent the afternoon in our tiny hotel room sketching the pictures with six colored pencils.

The next morning when we knocked on doors, we offered to show pictures that tell "good news." The response was amazing;

everyone wanted to see the pictures. Mothers called their children and neighbors to gather round. They listened attentively, often standing in the hot sun. They asked good questions. Some invited us back to show it to their husbands.

Pastor Peter Mathiasen, however, saw the possibility of the flip chart as an aid for our lay members to share the gospel with others. While he was on home assignment in Canada in 1963, a member of his church taught him the silk screening process so he could mass-produce the flip charts in Brazil.

On Mathiasen's return as parish pastor in Cianorte, we initially produced fifty sets of the colored charts. We prepared a how-to guide on using it to share the good news. Pastor Louis Becker, head of our mission publishing house, printed our revised and expanded version of the booklet and published subsequent editions of the flip chart.

Vili still keeps his flip chart in his briefcase so it is always handy for sharing the good news. When he speaks in churches, he asks if anyone would like a home visit for a family presentation of *O Abismo Ligado*.

That afternoon I was like the woman at the well who in her excitement left her water pot (John 4). I was no longer concerned about my cup of coffee. I was deeply moved to think that something we had prepared almost thirty-five years before, which I had completely forgotten about, was still being used in Brazil to share the gospel and bring people to faith.

## GOOD MANNERS

When the street car suddenly jerked, Ruth Aamot found herself sitting on a young man's lap. She flashed him a smile but instead of saying, *"Desculpe-me,"* excuse me, she said, *"Com licença,"* with your permission.

# An Investment That Paid Off

*Jack Aamot*

My friend Jim was counseling me to begin a one-to-one ministry with a core group of men. But how could I afford to invest time with one person when my workload was already so heavy? It not only seemed impossible but a poor use of time.

I originally had been called to be youth pastor in the ten thousand-member Church of the Ascension in Novo Hamburgo. Now I had not only been left as the only pastor to minister in this huge parish, but people were being converted and cell groups formed.

In December 1964, I had moved my wife, Ruth, and three young sons from a small mission congregation in north Paraná to this shoe manufacturing city in the southernmost state, Rio Grande do Sul. Our mission had sent me in response to invitations to provide pastoral assistance to large congregations of the Evangelical Church of the Lutheran Confession in Brazil (IECLB). I was young both in age and experience.

Beside youth work, I would help the sixty-five-year-old German pastor with general pastoral duties. Two months later he left for vacation in Germany. The load got heavy, but we knew it would last for only a few months. Then word came that he had retired and would stay in Germany. I was alone in this traditional parish of 3,500 families with its large number of weddings, funerals, and confirmation classes.

I was encouraged by increased worship attendance, however, as I preached about the necessity for a personal, experiential relationship with Jesus.

At the same time the congregation was launching a stewardship program that, for the first time in their one hundred year history, entailed members visiting families to explain Christian stewardship and to receive a financial pledge instead of collecting church dues.

A significant breakthrough came when I challenged the visitors to share their faith openly and winsomely with the people they visited. Many realized they had nothing to share and asked how they could know for sure that they really had this personal relationship with Jesus.

At one training session eleven stewardship visitors invited Christ into their lives as Savior and Lord. We immediately formed them into a small group for their growth and nourishment.

As they grew week by week and shared their faith, others came to a living faith, and we formed new ECO groups. ECO, Portuguese for echo, was coined from the first letter of three words that caught the purpose and format: *estudar,* to study; *compartilhar,* to share; and *orar,* to pray. They became exciting echoes of what God was doing both in and through them.

The success of these two principles—a clear sharing of the gospel, which led to discovering new life in Christ, and the cell group to study, share, and pray together—created my desperate need for help in effectively leading this growing number of Christians without neglecting the traditional pastoral ministry.

That's when I consulted Jim Petersen, a Navigator missionary in Brazil. Jim pointedly challenged me to train faithful and able men and women, on a one-to-one basis, as the apostle Paul had done with Timothy, his son in the faith (2 Timothy 2:2). I was very unsure that I could afford to spend time with only one person when other demands on my ministry were so heavy.

Ruth joined me in prayer to see if God would so lead. Within three days, five men individually approached me to request meeting with them on a one-to-one basis!

With this clear indication from God, we began the third step in what was to become a renewal movement across the Brazilian Lutheran Church—the training of laypeople in the leadership of spiritual multiplication, as Paul did with Timothy.

As God blessed us with phenomenal growth in attendance and outreach, other pastors and laypeople came to ask, "What's going on?" I soon began to meet with five pastors, also on a one-to-one basis, to introduce them to what became known as the "three-legged stool" concept:

- A personal experience of Jesus with assurance of salvation
- Disciplined growth through participation in cell groups
- The training of the laity through one-to-one contacts

These three principles became the foundation for a renewal movement that later was officially organized and registered as *Movimento Encontrão* (Encounter Movement).

As cell groups sprang up in different towns and states, the Novo Hamburgo congregation hosted the first larger gathering (Encontrão) in 1967. Thirty years later, a dozen or more regional rallies are held annually.

The third national gathering, held in Joinville, Santa Catarina, in February 1996, brought together over 3,700 laypersons and pastors for five days of spirited worship, serious study, and warm fellowship. Seventy percent were young people. It was the largest gathering of Lutherans (IECLB) in the history of Brazil.

The Encounter Movement has established, with the support of the IECLB, the Pastoral and Mission Center *(Centro de Pastoral e Missão)* in Curitiba, offering a three-year course for the biblical, theological, and missionary training of laypeople.

Another outgrowth of the Encounter Movement within the IECLB is Zero Mission *(Missão Zero)*. A pastor and selected families move to an area where there are no Lutheran churches or families, find employment, and serve as the nucleus for developing a new mission, using the "three-legged stool" concept.

God dramatically demonstrated to me that one-to-one nurture and training is never a waste of time but a wise investment of kingdom resources with ongoing dividends. It launched a renewal movement within the IECLB that three decades later continues to evangelize, nourish, and equip many thousands.

### GLASSES TO GLASSES, DUST TO DUST

My first contact with my new congregation was a funeral that I and others would never forget. Ruth and I were visiting Bob and Alona Roiko for a few days in the Rio Negro-Mafra parish since they were preparing to return to the States. We would soon be assuming this parish.

Bob asked me to take the funeral of an older member.

Unfortunately, I had placed my new reading glasses in my jacket pocket. As I leaned back in the seat of the car, I heard them snap—broken at the nose bridge. Fortunately, I had Scotch tape, so I wrapped them together.

Ruth and I, with a few family members, squeezed around the coffin in the small living room. We announced a hymn, but I heard only Ruth and myself singing. In the middle of the song, I could feel my glasses slipping apart as the tape melted from the heat of the day. I was immobilized as both hands were full, holding Bible, liturgy book, and hymnal. Suddenly one half of the glasses fell into the open coffin, on the body of the deceased. The other half clung to my face.

In true Brazilian hospitality, the brother of the deceased took off his glasses and slipped them on me. They were of no help. Somehow I sang to the end of the hymn.

I winged my way to the end of the service, knowing that the family was having as hard a time controlling their laughter as their new pastor was.

—Ray Holter

# A Window of Opportunity

*Andrew Olsen*

Pastor Clifford Biel and I often teamed up for evangelistic meetings in our northern part of Paraná State. He had a generator in the back of his Jeep station wagon, and we fired up a public address system. We showed 16 millimeter evangelistic movies to people, many of whom had never been in a theater. In the mid-1960s, television had not yet been introduced in these frontier areas still lacking electricity. Much to the surprise of these traditional Lutherans, we accompanied the singing with my accordion and Cliff's violin.

During a week's series in Cidade Gaúcha, a strong Germanic Lutheran community, people sardine-packed into the church building rather than stand outside in the heavy rainstorms. This presented a problem—we could not get through the crowd from the entrance of the church where we ran the projector. In order to speak to the congregation face-to-face, Cliff and I had to lay decorum aside and enter and exit by crawling through a window in the altar area. The window was four feet from the floor. If you wish to visualize our doing this, you must know that Cliff and I were among the largest of our colleagues and towered over most Brazilians.

I was the first non-German speaking pastor to serve this congregation of Lutherans who had migrated north from Rio Grande do Sul in search of new land and a new life. I had the privilege of being the first to teach and preach in Portuguese to these determined pioneers.

Part One: They Hear the Word and Accept It

One evening of the evangelistic series was especially memorable because Oscar Klug, a dormitory student from the mission high school in Cianorte where I had been director, was in attendance. But more important, that evening Oscar's dad had brought his non-German speaking farm workers to hear the presentation of the gospel. It was the first time people of non-Germanic ancestry had worshiped in that church. I'm sure it became a topic of conversation in many homes of that congregation. There was literally and figuratively a window of opportunity for the gospel in Cidade Gaúcha.

### A JOB FOR BILLY GRAHAM

On arrival in Brazil, we attended a language school that included orientation to Brazilian culture. One teacher stressed how we women, as *donas de casa,* homemakers, must interact politely but firmly with our *empregadas,* our household help, so that we could remain in control of our own home.

I thought this was good advice, so one day I decided to tell our *empregada* to clean the oven. But instead of the word for oven, *forno,* I said *inferno,* the word for hell.

She smiled, repeated the word, and asked, "Are you sure?"

I responded as sternly as I could, "Yes, I certainly am. Clean out the *inferno* today!" Then I realized my error, and we both burst out laughing.

She confessed she might have had trouble obeying that order. I no longer worried about maintaining control.

—Janel Hetland

# The Bottom Line

*George Knapp*

It was decision time—would we or would we not continue our sideline ministry that had started so well but fizzled to zero participation? No one but our own family had come for Sunday school and worship. The bottom line was zero. We had to make our first decision—to proceed with the planned lessons and worship for that day or not. We did. Then, more importantly, would we offer it again next Sunday for the community?

After all, this was a ministry my wife, Helen, and I were conducting alongside of our official work as houseparents at the Londrina hostel for MKs: missionary kids. No one would fault us for attending the church in town with the twenty-some children for which we were responsible. It would give us a change of scenery, and we could enjoy the ministry of others.

But there were so many people surrounding our campus on the edge of town who also needed the gospel and could not make the long trip to the center of town.

We had begun when the MKs were gone for an extended school vacation by holding a vacation Bible school that grew from twenty to about fifty children. They were so enthusiastic; many came an hour before starting time to make certain they didn't miss out on anything.

From this good start, attendance at Sunday school and worship was encouraging. After a while, however, it began to dwindle until that Sunday when only our family attended.

We decided that since it couldn't get any lower, it could only increase. So we continued. The next Sunday, with two more in attendance, we had a 200 percent increase! Thereafter it increased steadily.

Eighty-five children attended the last vacation Bible school during our term as houseparents. Every morning they lined up before entering the chapel in orderly fashion. The line stretched from the chapel to half way around the large hostel building. Again, many were coming nearly an hour early.

From this group we remember Antônio, who, with his widowed mother and sister, found salvation in Christ and were regular attendees. There was also João Marques, who later had a small congregation meeting in his own home. Valdemar and his family of four children discovered the change Christ could bring to their lives.

We do not know where they are today and what resulted from our sideline ministry from December 1962 to April 1965. The bottom line, however, is not numbers but God's faithfulness. We trust that God has used the Word that was planted in good soil.

## CHULÉ NO. 5

Don Nelson, instead of asking the butcher for a kilo of *concho mole,* beef fillet, asked for *chulé,* the filth accumulated between unwashed toes and the stench of perspiring feet.

# The Long Road to Faith

*Otto C. Tollefson*

A long time was needed for me to finally open my heart to Jesus," said retired bank manager Ibarir Cordeiro. "It wasn't because I was an atheist or an agnostic but only because I didn't know the Bible and its truth."

Ibarir and his wife, Ilka, told their story of coming to faith in Christ at the board meeting of International Lutheran Marriage Encounter and its North American Region's Family Reunion, both in St. Louis, July 1997.

Ibarir was born to a very poor couple in a small town in the interior of Santa Catarina State. Very early he had to work hard to pay for his schooling. Even though he had not finished elementary school, he felt confident that he knew enough to live his life the way he wanted.

At the age of thirteen, together with a friend, he opened a successful *churrascaria,* barbecue restaurant, in the center of town. Even though his capital was small, his knowledge of the business and self-confidence were great.

When the time came to serve in the military, he embraced it enthusiastically as an opportunity to learn something new and, with a little luck, perhaps rise to the rank of general. His self-confidence was high.

He was first stationed in the small town of Rio Negro, Paraná. He set up housekeeping with some military buddies in the basement of an ice cream parlor operated by a single mother and grandmother.

"It was there that God had reserved for me my better half, Ilka," Ibarir said. "She was a beautiful girl, sweet and hard-working—only eight years old at that time."

A few years later the whole battalion was moved to Minas Gerais State. But once a year Ibarir took the twenty-three hour bus ride back to Rio Negro to visit Ilka. He took many training courses and rose to the rank of sergeant. This dream fulfilled soon became a disappointment because the only position open for his rank in the whole country was on the frontier, in the Amazon jungle, which had no infrastructure. Ibarir didn't want mosquitoes and snakes.

Although he had traveled a lot throughout Brazil in his short military career, he thought it best to change the course of his life. He began another career totally different from what he had planned and dreamed for himself.

"The idea of being a bank employee, handling money, fascinated me," he explained, "and to use a suit and tie would be elegant!" He approached it with his usual self-confidence.

But the time was coming for him to make the most serious decision of his life. Ibarir said, "It would be to share my closet and brush my teeth with someone who certainly was waiting for that moment." He was twenty-eight; Ilka was eighteen and waiting! Robert Roiko, a missionary pastor, married them on March 6, 1971, in the church Ilka had attended sporadically.

Ibarir recalled, "Finally the great day came, and there we were in the presence of God and among our family and friends. Ilka was even more beautiful in her wedding gown and long veil. I confess that for the first time in my life, I was feeling very emotional. At the same time, I was a little afraid of what I could do to make her happy. But I was ready to dedicate the love I had in my heart to this woman."

Ibarir always gave his best to his banking career. It didn't matter how much work had to be done. What was really important was that he be a successful professional man. The promotions and awards were many and constant.

When the bank directors offered him a very attractive position that entailed moving to Curitiba, the capital of the state of Paraná, he confidently accepted the challenge.

As time went by, their children, Simone and Jeyson, were growing up and involved in their own activities. As a couple, their lives became a monotonous routine; their relationship stagnated. There was little communication but much misunderstanding. Ibarir stayed away from home as much as possible, investing his energy in his work.

By 1984, everything indicated that their marriage was ending. After Ilka asked Ibarir if he wanted a separation, they finally had a serious and frank discussion. They decided to give themselves another chance. Then Ilka surprised him with the news that she was pregnant.

"And now I can see the way God works," Ibarir reflected, "changing our plans for a separation to preparing a home for Karina, our third child."

Little did they know how their lives would be changed when two years later they had to move again, against his will. Ibarir explained, "We were living very comfortably in Curitiba, but I had to accept a position in a town that I didn't know and didn't want to know—Joinville, an industrial city in the state of Santa Catarina."

Soon after their arrival, one of Ibarir's co-workers, Ilídio, and his wife, Hilde, invited them to attend a Lutheran Marriage Encounter weekend. Ibarir remembers asking them, "And just why should we go there?"

Ilídio gently explained that it could make their good marriage better. But Ibarir, ever the self-confident one, did not agree that it was needed because in his judgment their marriage was stable enough. But Ilka insisted on attending.

Now Ibarir says, "It was the best experience I have ever had. We had been married then for seventeen years, and never had we talked about so many important things for our relationship.

"We experienced a wide range of emotions, and afterward I really opened my heart to let Jesus into my life. From then on I dedicated myself to studying God's Word and began to understand so much I had never even noticed before.

"Through the Lutheran Marriage Encounter many good things happened to transform our lives, but the most important was my relationship to God and my family."

They both agree that the Lord's hand was in the bank's unexpected decision to move them back to Curitiba where Ibarir finished his twenty-six-year career in banking.

This move made it possible for them to help bring Lutheran Marriage Encounter to that state. The Cordeiros are now co-lay executive couple for the South American region.

God's patience and grace had brought Ibarir from self-confidence to faith in Christ and to service toward others.


### BIGFOOT SLEPT HERE

Ruth and I were attending the churchwide assembly in Isabela, the site of the earliest Lutheran congregation in Santa Catarina State. More than a century later, however, neither electricity nor hotels had reached this village.

The delegates were overnight guests in the homes of a gracious community. A Roman Catholic family welcomed us to their immaculate but small home.

Our bed was so small that my six-foot, two-inch frame didn't fit. My feet were jammed against the footboard; my head propped at the headboard. We decided to lay the straw mattress on the floor, but it was still not possible for my entire body to be in the room. The solution was to put my feet in the hall under the curtain that served as a door.

I slept well but still wonder what the family thought about seeing their guest's big feet protruding into the hallway.

Ray Holter

# A Life Changed

*Jack Aamot*

A ten-year-old boy was playing with a truck in the dirt as I approached a simple home to clap at the gate, announcing my arrival. His name was Douglas. We chatted for awhile. Then I invited his mother to attend our meetings. She accepted the invitation and became a faithful worshiper.

It was the early 1960s; our mission work was in its initial phase in the wild west of Brazil's frontier movement. Peter Mathiasen was helping me open a small ministry in the town of Alto Paraná, less than ten miles from Paranavaí, my parish center. We had rented a corner storefront, had benches built, and, going door to door, had started to invite people to our evening services.

About five years later, a young teenager attending high school in Paranavaí heard of the American preacher and attended one of our services to check it out and maybe learn a little conversational English. It was the same Douglas.

By the work of the Holy Spirit, Douglas Wehmuth heard the gospel and accepted Christ as his Savior. Ruth and I gave him special attention, and he enjoyed his time in our home.

A few years later when we moved south to Novo Hamburgo, we invited Douglas to live with us and to attend school. His mother had passed away, and he didn't have adequate support to continue his studies in Paranavaí.

Eventually Douglas attended a school to become a catechist. Later he studied at the theological seminary in São Leopoldo and was ordained a pastor in the Evangelical Church of the Lutheran Confession in Brazil (IECLB). Today he serves a church in the port city of Porto Alegre. He is a vital part of the leadership of the Movimento Encontrão, the renewal movement within the IECLB.

When my colleagues and I evaluate the early work of our mission in the interior of Paraná, we include Douglas as one of the many whose lives were touched and transformed by God.

## Lessons Not Caught in Language School

Miss Toshiko Arai, our Japanese missionary, came to Paranavaí by bus from Cianorte where she lived. Then, because it was considerably cheaper than the Jeep taxi, she took a horse-drawn cart from the bus station to our house. Finally I decided I had to tell her that those carts were for prostitutes and their customers! She was appalled, thinking that she may have caused a scandal. But I assured her that we were not compromised, only ridiculed as foreigners who have so much to learn.

Then, out of sincere concern for being a good witness, she asked me to tell her what else she did that might be an embarrassment. I explained that her habit of making the OK sign, touching the tip of her forefinger to the thumb, is an obscene sign in Brazil.

—Andrew Olsen

# Saved by the Cross

*Janel Hetland*

A single gunshot punctured the silence. The startled congregation jumped to their feet, although it might have been wiser to drop to the floor. The bullet shattered the window between the visiting organist, Sheila Olander, and my husband, Glenn, who was presiding at the evening service.

The pastors and men of the congregation cautiously attempted to find the gunman. When no one could be found hiding under the cover of darkness, we decided it was safe to continue the service.

Pastor Ed and Sheila Olander had joined us for a series of evangelistic services in the little church we were serving in Paraná. This area was then known as Brazil's frontier. The gunshot that night reinforced our image of it being similar to the American Wild West we had only read about or seen in movies.

That evening, Alicia,* who had recently become a Christian, returned home to a drunken husband. Sabastião was furious that she had gone to church and wasn't home to fix his supper.

He admitted to her that he had gone to church planning to kill her. He had aimed at Alicia, but as he was pulling the trigger, he saw the cross on the altar and inadvertently moved the gun slightly. After firing the one shot, he decided to wait for her at home. Although he was still very angry, he didn't attempt to shoot Alicia in the home. Instead, he viciously beat her.

When Alicia did not attend services the next evening, and we learned what had happened to her, Glenn decided we should visit the family. This would not be easy because they lived in a very remote area. With every step I was ready to retreat, but Glenn insisted we had to talk to this family. I did not relish an armed confrontation with an angry husband. My heart was pounding like a jackhammer as we crawled through a barbed wire fence surrounding their house. We got to their home, and we did visit them. We left unharmed.

That evening the whole family was in church. Much to the surprise of everyone, when an invitation was given to respond to the good news, Sabastião went to the altar, knelt before the cross, and prayed. The next evening his adult son, Jorge, responded in the same manner.

They attended the services as a family for the rest of the week and began worshiping on Sundays.

I marveled how quickly a life could be transformed and an attitude could be changed. It was a good lesson for me as a new missionary not to place anyone outside the saving power of the cross of Christ.

---

\*     The names have been changed.

# What Must We Do to Be Saved?

*Viola Reed*

In a letter dated November 4, 1958, from Cianorte, Paraná

Last Sunday the Lord particularly blessed our Sunday school when practically all the kids in my class accepted Jesus as Savior. Their ages range from about ten to over fourteen. In other words, confirmation age.

I couldn't quite believe this was actually happening to the whole roomful of kids. I did my best to send them down for closing exercises at the end of the class period, explaining that only those were to stay who really wanted to leave their sins, never to commit them again, and to give their lives to the Lord, to live only for him. Only a couple left, and the rest wouldn't budge. They wanted to be saved and that was that.

After at least three futile attempts to send them away, I sent word down for Ruth [Kasperson] to come up and help me with the job. We don't like to deal with a whole group at once. (I guess we're good Lutherans!) So Ruth went to one room and I to another, calling the kids in one by one.

Those who were waiting remained deathly still even without anyone around to hush them! They all seemed to know what their sins were and confessed them unhesitatingly. What a joy it was to see the light break through when they claimed salvation by faith!

We have a happy bunch of willing little school kids around these days . . . I'm convinced that salvation makes a greater change in the lives of youth than it does in older folks.

### GOD'S WATCHFUL CARE

I was returning alone from an evening house meeting in Cruzeiro do Oeste, in the heart of the western movement. The hour was late. I wanted to get back to Cianorte and home, so it was pedal to the metal in my Volkswagen Kombi. This was usually very necessary on the loose, sandy roads of Paraná that wound through the jungle and newly planted coffee fields. To slow down or stop often meant to be stuck.

I was coming around a curve at top speed when I saw the tree lying across the road. There was no way I could stop, so again, pedal to the metal, and *plunk . . . plunk,* the Kombi was over the tree, and I was happily on my way.

The next day I told Francisco Cavalcanti, a presbyter, about the incident. He looked at me with concern and said, "You don't understand what was going on, do you?"

"What do you mean?" I asked.

"Robbers," he replied. "Robbers cut down a tree so it falls across the road, and when a vehicle stops, they rob the driver, kill him, take his car, and disappear into the night."

I thought, *How very true! This dumb missionary surely needed the Lord's protecting hand.* I have wondered how many other times the Lord protected me without my awareness of it. I praise the Lord for such watchful care.

—Robert Kasperson

# Margarida's Nunc Dimittis

*Clifford Biel*

When I knew him, Frederico was already in his 80s. He had emigrated to Brazil from Germany before World War II. He was poor but proud; a musically gifted, well-educated German. And he was very bitter toward both the Evangelical and Catholic churches.

But Frederico and I had many interesting conversations. One in particular I remember vividly. I had returned from a retreat where about half the participants were Catholic and the other half a mixture of Protestants. All of the participants, however, were friendly towards charismatic renewal. It was my practice to visit Frederico regularly and tell him about these meetings and other positive things happening in the church. Gradually his bitterness gave way to a kind of grief-filled longing for the church as truly "Church."

When I told him about one of these retreats, he told me this story:

"I was a young man when I attended a school for deacons in Germany. One day a fellow student came to me and said, 'Frederico, you are a student of languages. You must come to Margarida's room tonight while she is saying her prayers. Something very strange is happening with her.

"So I went. Margarida was a poor girl from the interior of Germany with limited education. She was studying to be a deaconess.

At the hour of her bedtime she was lying on her back, in bed. Several students were watching her with curiosity. Ignoring them she closed her eyes, folded her hands, and prayed, "Dear Lord Jesus, I know that I am going to die soon; but please take care of my mama and my papa and my brothers and sisters." Then she began to sing. It was very beautiful, but I didn't understand the words.

"The next day I went to the director of the school, who was much more of a student of languages than I was. I told him about Margarida. The next evening we were both there, along with other curious students. Oblivious to all of us, she prayed once again and concluded as before. Once again she began to sing; it was very beautiful!

"The director said, 'Oh! I know that language. She's singing in Aramaic, the language Jesus spoke.'

"That night Margarida died. I went to the pastor and told him about Margarida, and I asked him, 'Pastor, what does it mean?'

"'Oh,' he shrugged, 'it doesn't mean anything.'

"But all these years I've wondered, *Did it mean something?*"

Not very long after that, Frederico became terminally ill. As I visited him on his deathbed, I shared with him the Word and then prayed the Lord's Prayer. In a very tired voice he joined in the "Amen". Then he lifted his arm, as though it were a very heavy weight, and let it fall four times in the sign of the cross over his tired, old body. He died that night.

# Part Two

## They Bear Fruit

# Kidnapped—and the Pastor Drove the Getaway Car

*Louis O. Becker*

How did I, a missionary pastor, become a kidnapper's accomplice? It all began soon after my family and I arrived in the small town of Cianorte in the coffee producing area of north Paraná. One of my first pastoral acts was to perform an emergency baptism for the newborn son of José and Maria Fernandes.* He died a few hours later.

The loss of their firstborn child was a heavy blow to these teenage parents. José worked as a laborer on a large coffee farm as Maria had also done on her father's small farm before they were married. It had been a hasty marriage after her father discovered she was pregnant by "that ungodly lout from the plantation." Her parents, faithful members of our church, had hoped that she would wait until she was of proper age and then marry some nice Christian man. But Maria had a mind of her own, and she knew what she wanted.

Now, with the death of their child, all those wonderful dreams of a happy family with laughing children came crashing down. The doctor delivered another blow as he explained that the death of their son was because of Maria's poor health. "You must not become pregnant again," he warned. "You are anemic and too frail to bear more children."

Outwardly Maria accepted this new calamity with grace and proper resignation, but inwardly she was seething with anger and desperation. *How can God do this to me? How can my family accept it so easily? It isn't right! Why should others be the happy mothers of beautiful children and I go childless? No, it's not right, and it's not going to be so. I'll show them. I'll have my child after all!*

A plan began to take shape. Maria had no doubt it would fulfill all her desires. A few months after the death of the son, a quiet but determined Maria announced, to the consternation of her family and friends, that she was pregnant again. This was the initial step in her desperate plan.

About this time her older sister also became pregnant and became a perfect model for Maria. Week by week she added more padding to her stomach, accompanying the development of her sister, all the while proclaiming that she felt just fine and that the doctor was also quite satisfied with her state of health.

On a regular basis Maria announced to her neighbors in the dingy row of houses on the coffee farm that she was going into town to see her doctor. But she never did consult him. It was all part of her grand deception that went undetected for eight months. We saw Maria occasionally when she came to visit her parents during the evening services we held in their humble farm home. But we saw her only in the dull glow of a kerosene lantern.

The delivery date drew near. Maria again announced to her neighbors that she was going to the clinic alone by bus. Upon arriving in town, she found an isolated spot where she removed and disposed of the padding from under her dress. *I won't need that anymore, not after today!* she thought.

After making her way to the hospital, she cautiously entered the maternity ward to begin the selection process. Most of the infants were housed in rooms with their mothers, who, with family help, were expected to care for their own newborns.

Maria found one that was suitable, a boy with light brown skin like her own. She engaged the mother in small talk and graciously offered help in the feeding, rocking, and changing of the baby.

# Part Two: They Bear Fruit

"The room next door is empty," Maria announced to the mother. "If you don't mind, I'll just take the baby there for some tea and you can rest here in quiet." (It is an accepted practice among Brazilian mothers to give sweet, weak tea to their infants.)

The mother agreed hesitantly. Quickly Maria was out the side door of the hospital. She hurriedly walked down the street. So easy! Now, how was she to return home? Maria could not afford a taxi, and she did not want to wait hours for the bus. Then she remembered Toshiko, the woman missionary from Japan, and Pastor Louis from America. Both had cars. Surely one of them would help her.

Toshiko was in the middle of a women's Bible study but called me to ask if I could take the young mother and baby home. I knew of Maria's pregnancy and of her parents' concern with her weak physical condition.

"Certainly," I agreed. "I can leave right away." I was eager to be of help.

I expressed my surprise to Maria over the birth of the baby, not having heard anything from her parents whom I saw every week. Maria, however, spilled out the explanation that her parents did not know about the birth yet; it had all come about quite remarkably that morning as she was in the clinic. She described how she had rested for a few hours and did not have the money to stay over. She felt just fine, and the doctor had said it was OK. She would have plenty of help at home, and she would like to get there as soon as possible.

Driving very carefully over ten miles of rutted dirt roads, I joyfully delivered mother and baby. Shrieks of delight greeted Maria as she stepped from my car with baby in arms. Neighboring mothers and children crowded around for a peek. All pitched in to make mother and child comfortable.

Meanwhile, I was feeling extremely satisfied with my Good Samaritan role and even offered to take the long way home in order to inform Maria's parents of the blessed event. They were overjoyed to hear the good news and immediately made plans to walk the several miles to see their new grandson. They thanked me profusely for helping in such a generous way.

"God has been very good to us today," I said, not suspecting that the next day might bring a different assessment of these events.

The next morning Toshiko was having her hair done in a beauty salon. All the talk was about a kidnapped baby. "Yes, can you imagine? A farm girl with light brown skin made friends with the mother and then took the baby and just disappeared!"

Toshiko interrupted her hair procedure to make an urgent call. "Pastor Louis, have you heard about the kidnapping of a baby? Do you think it could be Maria?"

Whatever Good Samaritan feelings I had quickly evaporated. They were replaced by the floundering feelings of a Peter who had tried to walk on water only to end up crying, "Lord, save me!" I pictured myself before a relentless district attorney. "And now, Mr. American Missionary, did you or did you not transport this kidnapper and baby to her home? Do you expect this jury to believe that you were hoodwinked by this obviously fabricated story of a surprise birth?"

Even if I were exonerated of collaboration, I would emerge either as totally naive or utterly stupid.

I called the hospital to arrange for a nurse who might identify the baby to accompany me to the home of Maria and José. It was a painful pastoral visit. They reluctantly agreed to allow the baby to be brought back to the hospital for identification, all the time insisting that he was their son.

On the trip into town my mind was still picturing the judicial process of the United States and the merciless probing of the media. But this was rural, interior Brazil. Fortunately, only the police were waiting. They kindly but firmly questioned the accused couple who eventually made a full confession.

The grateful parents were so happy to have their baby back, they did not press charges. They wanted neither publicity nor revenge because they too were poor farmers, they explained.

After a stern lecture from the chief of police, and being put on his personal probation list, the guilty pair was released. No trial, no jail term, no fine, and little publicity.

"Thank you, Lord!" I sighed. "The Lord has been good to us today!"

Although the young couple had made matters right with the baby's parents and the civil authorities, all was not yet right with God.

The following Sunday afternoon I made another pastoral visit to Maria and José with the invaluable help of Maria's father. My Volkswagen bus served as the counseling chamber, out of sight and sound from inquisitive neighbors.

At first there was denial of guilt, and then each one blamed the other. But in the end there were tears of repentance and prayers of confession, followed by the declaration of forgiveness for sinners from God who gave his Son to die for all our human folly.

I could only thank God for showing me that once again, through his mercy, all things do work out for good.

---

\* The names have been changed.

# The Prayer of Faith Will Save the Sick Man

Odin Kenneth Stenberg

L ate one night, about a year after my family arrived in Juiz de Fora, Senhor João, the one black elder in the village of Borboleta, knocked at the door. João had an urgent request. "It's my neighbor, Senhor Petermann," he said. "You know he has been sick for a long time. Now the doctor says he has only twenty-four hours to live, and Petermann says you must come with the Extreme Unction." (Many of the Protestant religious practices in Brazil are blended with Catholicism.)

I threw my communion kit of wine and wafers into the briefcase, took Senhor João with me in my old Volkswagen Kombi, and drove across a foothill range to Vila Borboleta.

Petermann was indeed very ill: his long, gaunt body writhing on a mattress in the middle of the room. His emaciated face had turned a pale, yellowish pallor. His eyes were glazing over. He appeared to be in a coma.

Selecting a passage I had often used at a sickbed, I read from the Book of James: "Is there anyone who is sick? He should send for the church elders, who will pray for him, and rub olive oil on him in the name of the Lord. This prayer made in faith will heal the sick person; the Lord will restore him to health, and the sins he has committed will be forgiven" (James 5:14,15 TEV).

With the elder kneeling beside me, I spoke to the unconscious form lying there before us. Although I had a feeling of futility in doing it, I carefully explained the need for repentance and confession so that the man might receive the promised forgiveness. And the elder reviewed the promises: "Though your sins are like scarlet, they shall be like snow; though they are red like crimson they shall become like wool" (Isaiah 1:18 NRSV).

I put the wafer into the sick man's mouth, and a little wine. The elder prayed and I followed, laying my hand on the body, as I usually did when I ministered to the sick. I focused mainly on the family gathered around the bed—a very poor family that would soon be destitute. I prayed that their needs might be met.

Just before closing, and as an afterthought, I added, "And Lord, if it is your will that our brother be made well and be restored to his family, your will be done." I closed with the words of the Benediction, "The Lord bless you and keep you. . . ."

Giving each one in the family a final hug, I bid them goodnight and drove back to the city to get a few hours sleep.

The next day I left with my wife, Carola, and family for a mission conference a considerable distance away, in the interior of Paraná. We were there for two weeks. On the way back I stopped off at São Paulo for a day of meetings with the pastors of my district. One pastor from a city near my parish took me aside and told me that two of my members had died in my absence.

I thanked him for presiding at the funerals and thought briefly about who these members may have been. I knew Mrs. Salzer, ninety years of age, had long awaited her death. The other, of course, would be Petermann, the man to whom Senhor João and I had given the final communion.

I boarded a bus for an all-nighter back to Juiz de Fora. I rested a little before going to the Salzer home. There I found that Dona Salzer had died. Her daughter was there alone, waiting for me. After reading from the Psalms, I prayed with her and held her while she sobbed out her grief.

Then I drove across the range into Vila Borboleta. I stopped at the bamboo gate before the Petermann house and, as was the custom, clapped my hands to announce my presence. Tired by the long bus ride, I looked absentmindedly down the street.

A moment later I was shocked wide awake by a familiar voice. Turning to determine who it may be, I saw a man striding toward me with a broad smile on his ruddy face. The man flung open the gate and threw his arms around me in a bone-crushing embrace.

It was Petermann. And it was the surprise of a lifetime! His wife, Dona Julia, said, "In the twenty-four hours after you and João had left his bedside, my man began to recover!"

News of the healing raced through the village, down the valley to the other towns and communities. I could not say it brought a lot more people into the church, but I met a new friendliness: frequent smiles of acceptance and respect on the streets and along the trails of the countryside.

---

* Edited from the unpublished novel, *Islands on a Wide Sea*, by Odin Kenneth Stenberg. Copyright 1997. Used by permission.

# God's Perfect Timing

*Otto C. Tollefson*

I was both angry and feeling sorry for myself as I returned to a little hotel in downtown São Paulo. I had rushed to the airport only to discover that because of afternoon traffic I had missed the only plane back to Cianorte, Paraná. What a waste of taxi fare—and time. I had already spent two days attempting to find qualified evangelical teachers and houseparents for our new Lutheran school.

The opening of the residential high school in our frontier town was a few weeks away. I was burdened with supervising the final construction, purchasing equipment, handling bureaucratic documentation, and recruiting students and staff. The Lord should have known I didn't need to waste time in this huge metropolis.

As I dejectedly checked in at the same hotel I had left a few hours earlier, my eye caught the registration card on the counter for Elden Landvik, a missionary colleague.

"Is he here?" I asked excitedly. "I'll room with him!" The receptionist looked at me strangely and said Elden had just gone up in the elevator and that he'd call to verify if that were acceptable. It was. At least I wouldn't eat dinner alone.

Elden had just flown in from Presidente Prudente, in the interior of São Paulo State. He had a message for me: According to Eldon, Bob Maland, president of our mission, urgently wanted me to contact him. Bob had good news of a young Japanese woman as a possible replacement for Miss Kiyoko Suda who had been the founder and only teacher in our Japanese school on the frontier.

Kiyoko was leaving to pursue a nursing career. If it was difficult to find Brazilian evangelical teachers who would venture out to the wild west, where would I ever find a Christian teacher for Japanese children, one who could also evangelize the many immigrants and first generation Japanese?

Because I could not reach the Maland home by telephone, I decided that instead of returning directly to Cianorte, it would be best to fly to Marília, in the interior of São Paulo State. There I heard from Bob the most fascinating story of Shinobu, a Japanese woman in her early twenties.

I learned that Shinobu was the daughter of an evangelical pastor in Japan. She had felt the Lord calling her to Brazil to work among her people who were migrating to the new farmlands. In spite of the clear call, she wondered how she would ever be able to go. No mission would send her. Brazil was accepting only those Japanese who would come as agricultural workers. Furthermore, they had to come in family units. Shinobu was single; she was not a farmer; she had no promise of employment.

When another emigrating Christian family heard of her dilemma, they offered to adopt her legally as their daughter so she could go with them to fulfill God's call. She accepted the adoption offered her.

Like Abraham and Sarah of old (Hebrews 11:8), Shinobu obeyed in faith when God called her to go to a country that God had promised to give her. She left her native land, her relatives, and her father's home without knowing exactly where she was going.

That afternoon Bob Maland brought me to the farm where Shinobu was being hosted. Arrangements were made in a three-way language conversation: Shinobu, Bob, and I in English; her sponsor, Bob, and I in Portuguese; Shinobu and her sponsor in Japanese.

On the long bus ride back to Cianorte, I reflected on God's provision and timing. Months or years before we had asked, God had set the wheels in motion to provide a replacement for Kiyoko.

Far away in another state, Bob knew this sponsoring family and our need for a worker. He realized that a letter would take perhaps a month to reach us; we had no phone service in our frontier town. Fortunately he had passed the word on to Elden. If I hadn't missed the plane, if Elden had arrived earlier or later at the hotel, if the clerk had immediately filed Elden's registration card, I would have missed this timely opportunity.

Shinobu arrived in Brazil at the exact time we needed someone who could be both a teacher for our Japanese courses for immigrant children and an evangelism worker in our congregation. She was a blessing to our mission. A few years later she married a Japanese Free Methodist pastor, served in Brazil, and later, I heard, in the United States. I thank God for such amazing provision and perfect timing.

## ON FLIES AND GERMS

At times we overheard our frontier domestic help discussing with other Brazilians some of our strange ways, such as our having screens on our windows. "Why would those Americans want them?" they asked each other. "How could the flies and bugs in the house possibly get out?

"Or what about the ridiculous idea of something called microbes? The Americans say they are so tiny you can't see them and yet insist that these germs could cause dysentery, other illnesses, or even death. Imagine that!"

Or they'd say, "Those Americans are so strange—why, they boil their babies' bottles and even boil the water they give their babies. *Que coisa!* What a thing!"

—Ruth Kasperson

# Christmas in a New Land

*Mary Jo Peterson*

The lack of familiar cultural traditions could not stifle a feeling of excitement and expectancy as our family prepared to celebrate our first Christmas in Cianorte, Paraná. There was no cold weather, no snow, and in most homes, no decorated Christmas trees.

As our three children and I walked to the street market early Christmas Eve morning, we heard the squealing of young pigs being carried home to be roasted for Christmas dinners. Goats waiting to be sold bleated nervously. Nearly every stand in the market offered squawking live hens, tied by their legs to wooden poles.

As we strolled past crudely built stands, hopeful hawkers offered fresh fruits, toys, and homemade soap. One merchant unsuccessfully tried to sell us a pig's head for twenty-five cents. In the next stand a woman was marketing pigs' feet. In our family neither would substitute for Norwegian lutefisk.

With our shopping cart full, we were ready to return home but not before savoring some *pastéis* fried right before us in a huge skillet of hot oil. These pastries filled with cheese, hamburger, or hearts of palm were our favorite treat and would make a delicious fast-food dinner any day.

The excitement of Christmas built in the early afternoon as we gathered in our small church to practice music for the various Christmas services to be held over the next few days. I especially thought of the last service, which would be outdoors on a small farm a few days after Christmas. The light would come from the full moon and our kerosene lantern. We could expect sixty to seventy people. Each child would receive a small box of candy prepared by the Sunday school in Cianorte. We would present each worshiper with a pretty picture crafted from last year's Christmas cards. For some children, these simple gifts might be the only ones they received for Christmas.

Our hearts filled with thanksgiving for the privilege of being in a new land where we could share the wonderful story of the birth of Christ.

Finally, with rehearsals over and Christmas preparations completed in our home, it was time for some restful sleep. Christmas Eve had passed; Christmas Day would soon be upon us.

About two o'clock in the morning we were awakened by sounds of music wafting through our bedroom windows. Opening the shutters, we discovered carolers singing to us in their beautiful Portuguese language: *"Noite feliz! Noite feliz!"* ("Silent night! Holy night!") What a great way to begin Christmas Day! What a beautiful custom.

Even though it was hot, even though I could not purchase lutefisk at the market, even though we could not go to Grandma's house, God was with us in a new land. The birth of Jesus the Savior was as precious in Cianorte as it would be anywhere in the world.

We who had been excited about sharing such good news with the Brazilians were on the receiving end. Like the Bethlehem shepherds, we will never forget being awakened by angelic music in the wee hours of Christmas morning.

# A Heavenly Chorus

*Viola Reed*

(In a letter dated February 7, 1958, from Cianorte, Paraná)

For the first time since we came to Brazil, we went Christmas caroling. It was done a little differently from the way we do it in the United States. The choir members insisted on going in the morning—at daybreak or earlier—instead of in the evening. They wanted people to be awakened by these beautiful strains, and they declared that there'd be no object in our going at night. I like it better that way myself now that I've experienced it.

So, as the first rays of light streaked the eastern sky and the jungle began to awaken, we were on our way. Flashlights were necessary for reading the words, but the morning twilight is short in this country and we could soon dispose of them.

The reception: Some folks simply opened the shutters of their windows enough to better hear the words of "Silent Night" or "Joy to the World" or "Noel." Others came out to the gate and invited us in. The mayor was pleased as a child! We learned afterward that the school inspector had opened the window shutters and then had sat down and wept; for her the music compared with that of "a heavenly chorus"! I assure you we don't have much of a choir, but the Latins are a very emotional people. Nevertheless, the inspector came to the Christmas program the next night and has begun to show a renewed interest in the school!

# More Than a Seasonal Peace

*Ann Maland*

T hat's a house that I once wanted to flee from," Dona Irene exclaimed after I had shared my joy over the transformation that
had come to the Ivo Schmidt family.* I had seen the dramatic change
when we celebrated, by our choice, a nontraditional Christmas.

The sweltering December heat wave made it too hot to bake, so
ice cold watermelon, cool shrimp salads, and cold eggnog took the
place of baked and cooked foods from our Scandinavian heritage.

We went nontraditional all the way. Instead of our usual family
Christmas tree celebration on Christmas Eve, we made visits to
needy families and shut-ins.

We shared with the poor and sang carols with those less fortu-
nate. After seeing how even they made their simple preparations
in commemoration of the birth of the Savior, we sensed a greater
unity than ever with God's people. The significance of his coming
to earth, bringing hope for all people, seemed greater than ever.

The next Sunday evening, however, Dona Irene put it all into
perspective when we visited her and Senhor Edmundo in their
comfortable home following the congregation's Christmas program.
It was so beautifully decorated with an unusual Solomon's temple,
its interior illuminated with electric lights. A manger scene set up
in their living room witnessed to their faith.

I was telling Dona Irene how overjoyed I was with the changes I saw in the Ivo Schmidt family when we had visited on Christmas Eve. She too knew that the Schmidt family always had many problems, chiefly a lack of harmony, but also a fifteen-year-old hydrocephalic child, who, with the body of an infant, lay in a crib, unable to see or talk. They had several other children, including another exceptional, hyperactive ten-year-old. The father was often unemployed.

I shared how on my previous visit the main room in the home was downright filthy and the children repulsively dirty. But on Christmas Eve, the house was sparkling clean; there was new furniture. The family members were all beautifully clean, and, except for two children with a minor illness, all seemed genuinely calm and happy.

Dona Irene exclaimed, "Dona Ana, you just can't imagine what the Word of God has done to transform that family. That's a house that I once wanted to flee from, but when we resolved to divide our women's Bible study group into six neighborhood groups, I felt led by the Spirit to meet there.

"We had to borrow chairs from the neighbors to begin with," she continued, "but the older children have since contributed to purchasing a new table and chair set and a living room set. Senhor Ivo, who usually sat around doing nothing, always received a kind word or two of greeting from us, and he gradually warmed up and became very friendly. Now he's working and earning more that he ever had at any time in his series of odd jobs. A peace that they had never before experienced has come into their home."

I sensed it was more than a seasonal peace; it was a life transformation brought about by God's Word and the witness of caring people. We thank the Lord for Dona Irene who has found a deep satisfaction in sharing the Word, not only in the women's Bible study groups, but in other visits that she makes in her city.

The different situations that we encountered that nontraditional Christmas Eve spoke louder than any sermon, and we were unanimous: it is more blessed to give than to receive.

---

* The name has been changed.

# A Poet Waiting to Get Out*

*Peter E. Mathiasen*

Although Maria Edite Lederer had cerebral palsy, she danced along the road to the little one-room schoolhouse, moving with a rollicking gait and spastic jerks. She never would have been permitted in the schools of the big city, at least not then. But in that country school she came along with her cousin. Her education had stopped at the fifth grade. That's all they offered in the village of Quero Quero.

I met Maria when she was a preteenager. Together with her cousin, she enrolled in my first confirmation class in the Quero Quero schoolhouse, located two hours away from the congregation I served in Ponta Grossa, Paraná. At first I couldn't understand her garbled sounds without an interpreter. I soon discovered, however, that although she could not write, Maria knew all the answers.

When my family and I returned to Canada in 1975, she began to correspond with us by dictating to her cousin.

Then something life-changing happened to Maria. A second pastor was called to serve the large parish with over 650 families. This young pastor took an interest in Maria, and one day he brought her a present—a typewriter.

*Her cousin has learned to type,* I mused when I received her typewritten letter. It wasn't until the end of the letter that I learned that Maria herself had typed it. She couldn't write, but she could type! She had learned to express herself in the written word.

A new world opened for Maria. She began putting her thoughts on paper: what she saw in her backyard, observed in the world around her, and felt inside her.

Her writing had a poetic quality. This young woman with bent hands, muffled speech, and spastic mannerisms had a poet inside her waiting to get out.

Maria began to spend so much time at the typewriter that her parents complained she did little else. She became a regular contributor to the Brazilian Lutheran youth magazine and then the national church paper, writing the poetry she had closeted within her.

Maria determined to go back to school. With the help of members of the church in Ponta Grossa, she found a place to study. She persevered and has now graduated in English studies. During this time, she came to the attention of the State University of Ponta Grossa, which offered to publish her poetry in a book and gave her a gala party for the occasion. For the first time in her life, she spoke before a gathered group—yes, with her interpreter, this time the young pastor.

A second book of poetry was published in 1988. Then in 1991, the Synodical Publishing House of the Evangelical Church of the Lutheran Confession in Brazil published a collection of her poetry. A fourth book followed.

Maria became active with the youth of the church. She never misses a youth event or retreat. She visits local schools to talk with students, using an interpreter.

She was invited to participate in a youth exchange in Germany. When the sponsors learned she had cerebral palsy, they said it would be impossible for her to go along. Her whole group responded, "Then we won't go either!" The sponsors reversed their decision.

When she arrived in Germany, her host family gave her a camera, and she recorded the whole event on film.

Maria now uses a word processor in her writing. In a recent letter, Maria painted for me a word picture of her surroundings, describing the rustling leaves and blooming peach trees, the birds hopping from twig to twig under their canopy, with their expressive beaks and distinctive songs. She imagines them flying freely across fields, forests, cities, and oceans. She wrote:

> I think then of all of us as persons with our differences, our ways of thinking, acting, and being, of our social differences of culture, creed, and color. Yet like the birds, there is something which makes us equal, and which unites us, and makes us brothers and sisters in faith. It is our capacity to love. With the wings of this love we can cross great distances, minimize diversity, and unite with each other. Thanks be to God for the gift of being participants in the great heavenly family.

Her letter ends with a beautiful announcement. The pastor makes the trip to her village for worship only every other week. In the intervening weeks, the services are led by members. And Maria has been asked to write the sermons for these services!

The young girl who danced along the road to confirmation class in the village's one-room schoolhouse is now a poet of praise dancing the gospel into the lives of people.

---

\* Edited from *Poet of Praise*. Copyright by Peter E. Mathiasen. Used by permission.

# Me, Myself

*Maria Edite Lederer*

I could be
a beautiful red carnation
to decorate a living room
and be admired for my perfume.

I could be a majestic tree
with its massive trunk, spreading branches,
and green leaves,
a symbol of hope.

Perhaps a beautiful butterfly
with colorful wings in hues of blue or white or yellow,
decorating the beautiful spring.
Or who knows,
maybe a little bird,
flying in the azure sky,
singing out its liberty.

Or even the mysterious sea
with the calm ebb and flow of its waves,
washing the whitened beach.

## Part Two: They Bear Fruit

Or yet a joyful musical note,
bringing happiness to the sad ambience
of a lonely room.

But even if I'm not
a carnation's perfume, a majestic tree,
a beautiful butterfly, a bird set at liberty,
the mysterious ocean, or a joyful musical note,

I can be myself,
admired for who I am.
I can transmit hope through an extended hand,
decorate the spring of life with a smile,
have the liberty to think, dream, and be who I am,
reveal the mystery of life, and
know that my happiness is life itself.

And more important, being myself I can
love you and many others, and above all God.
God who made me who I am . . . *me!**

---

* From her first book, *A Little Bit of Me*. Translated from Portuguese by Peter
  E. Mathiasen. Copyright by Peter E. Mathiasen. Used by permission.

# They Forgave the Murderer

*Otto C. Tollefson*

The news of a murder and suicide spread like wildfire through our city of Joinville. The victims were two high school students, members of different parishes in our city.

As the pieces of the story came together that early morning, we learned that the evening before, as so often happened, Ivo had stopped by his girlfriend Nancy's home. He chatted with her parents, Senhor Evelino and Dona Lydia, and her two younger sisters as he helped with the supper dishes. Then he suggested to Nancy that they take a spin around town in his father's car before tackling their studies.

Hours passed and the two did not return. Fearing the worst, both families began a search that lasted throughout the night. The next morning their fully clothed bodies were found in Ivo's family cabin on the beach. Nancy was in a kneeling position with her head on the bed; Ivo, lying on the bed, had a revolver nearby. It was ruled that Ivo had murdered Nancy and committed suicide.

Separate funerals were scheduled for that afternoon. Before attending Nancy's funeral, we stopped to visit Ivo's distraught mother. Her husband was out of the country on business and could not return in time for the funeral. Alone, she sat asking, "Why did Ivo do it?"

Nancy's mother later told us that in those few hours before the funeral, she had been able to forgive Ivo for Nancy's death, but the *why* question had also persisted for her.

We knew Dona Lydia as a woman of faith but not one given to dreams and visions. We were surprised when she told us that the night after the funeral, when she finally fell asleep, Nancy had appeared at the foot of her parents' bed. With deep emotion she had pled, "Mother! Mother! Don't you understand? Ivo was sick! Mother, Ivo was sick!"

Dona Lydia explained, "I then remembered the deep emotional problems I had experienced years before, and I could understand why Ivo did it."

The day after the funeral, Senhor Evelino and Dona Lydia called on their pastor. "Everyone tells us that Ivo's parents must make the first move," they explained. "They insist that his parents should apologize to us and ask our forgiveness for what their son did to our Nancy."

"But Pastor," they asked, "even though we have never met his parents, can't we go to them now and tell them we have already forgiven Ivo and that we too sorrow over their son's death?" They went with no bitterness or malice to share in the pain that brought them together.

Subsequently they learned from Nancy's and Ivo's high school friends how he had vowed to kill her if she continued to insist on breaking off their relationship. His parents revealed that Ivo had been receiving professional treatment for psychological problems.

Dona Lydia believes that God had graciously answered her *why* question because she first used her God-given strength to forgive Ivo, as she herself had been so graciously forgiven throughout her lifetime.

The surprising news of their forgiveness and visit spread throughout the city almost as rapidly as had the tragic news two days before.

# She Didn't Want to Make That Kind of Money

*James L. Peterson*

Angela* came to our house on a lovely spring day just as Mary Jo and I had paused in midafternoon to enjoy a cup of coffee with hot milk. She was in the flower of her youth, as the saying goes—sixteen going on seventeen. She should have been cheerful on such a day with springtime in the air. But one look at her sad face and tears in her dark eyes was all that we needed to ask, "Why, Angela, what's wrong?" Her answer left us dumbfounded. Her father had made a shocking demand of her.

Paulo,* Angela's father, was a plumber—not a professional one, but more like a bargain plumber who does an okay job for a lot less money. He had been out of work for some time. He had many mouths to feed, and money was getting scarce. Angela's parents were members of our Evangelical Lutheran Church, but it was never easy for me, as their pastor, to get close to Paulo. He came to worship services, but when I tried to make eye contact with him, his carmel-brown eyes shifted a little. His look conveyed skepticism. Or could it be a look of resentment and jealousy toward us who were, in the eyes of many, the rich Yankees?

Between tears Angela poured out her story. That very morning, Paulo had demanded that she, as the oldest daughter, help support the family by quitting school and going to work in the *zona* for some quick cash! The *zona* was a little village, or zone, just outside the city where the prostitutes legally lived and worked. The family would live off the selling of her body to any buyer who came along.

Sadness clouded the otherwise beautiful day. We sat silent and speechless before this young woman so deeply hurt by a father who would demand such a demeaning job from his own flesh and blood.

That afternoon a prayer meeting of three gathered together in Jesus' name around our kitchen table. Jesus was with us, as he promised. We boldly asked for deliverance for our sister in the faith. God did provide a way. Angela determined she would not barter her body. She would refuse to obey her father in that which was degrading and morally wrong. The Spirit of Christ wiped away Angela's tears. God graciously saw her and her family through the difficult financial times.

Our anger was directed not only toward Paulo but toward poverty, a real monster in Brazil. We recognized more clearly the insidious immorality inherent in poverty in a land that boasts great material riches but so unjustly distributes them.

At the root of it all, we perceived a poverty of spirit. It led us to pray fervently: "Let me be neither rich nor poor. So give me only as much food as I need. If I have more, I might say that I do not need you. But if I am poor, I might steal and bring disgrace on my God" (Proverbs 30:8,9 TEV).

Waves of gratefulness surged through us for God's empowering grace as Angela returned home with the promise of spring in her eyes.

---

\* The names of Brazilians have been changed.

# Still Alive to Tell His Story

*Robert H. Fedde*

James Carlney, a twenty-five-year-old, half-Indian farmhand, looked so dark against the blond-haired adults and children of German ancestry who gathered for monthly worship services. As an orphan who had known neither father nor mother, he had experienced a series of traumatic events. Now he was a lonely laborer helping out at the farm that served as one of my twelve preaching places on Brazil's frontier with Paraguay.

At each service James gradually came to understand that there was hope for someone like him. His interest grew. Soon he was walking the nine kilometers to Cascavel to attend the 10:00 A.M. service on the Sundays when none were offered on the farm. He arrived an hour before worship to study with me the little booklet, *Salvation Made Plain,* originally published by the Lutheran Bible Institute.

One Sunday when James learned that the Cascavel congregation was having their annual Sunday school picnic and fall festival in a local park, he decided to stay and fellowship with his newfound family of faith. He was breaking out of his lonely shell.

As night was falling, he began the long walk home, first stopping at a drugstore to buy cold tablets. About four kilometers down the road where the jungle begins to form and the darkness of night closes in, he was attacked by three men with knives. They searched his pockets for money and found about three dollars; his satchel produced only his Bible and the study booklet. In disgust they tossed these to the ground, and, after beating him viciously, left in search of another victim. James stumbled the tortuous eight remaining kilometers to the farm.

Next Saturday James walked to Cascavel to tell me what had happened. As I listened, I silently wondered how this might negatively impact his newfound relationship with Christ. His final words dispelled my pastoral concerns: "Oh, how thankful I am that the Lord Jesus was near me and saved me so that I am still alive to tell the story of Jesus!"

## LITURGICAL STRIPTEASE

As in most of the established Lutheran churches in Brazil, it had not been the pastor's practice in the large church in downtown Curitiba to greet members at the door after the services. When I was invited to preach there, out of my desire to create a climate of friendliness, I intended to announce from the pulpit that I would greet the people at the door at the end of the service. I nearly brought the house down in uncontrollable laughter, however, when instead of saying I would go to the door to *me despedir,* to say goodbye, I said *me despir,* to strip naked!

—Richard Wangen

# Signs of Maturity

*Ann Maland*

Minutes and financial reports are seldom worth writing home about, let alone raising one's voice in thanksgiving for them. That evening, however, my heart began a silent song of gratitude as thirty-five women waited expectantly for the Christmas program of the women's auxiliary of the Caxias do Sul Evangelical Lutheran Church.

First, the Advent wreath was lit, then carols were sung in Portuguese. Dona Esther presented her meditation based on the idea of an end-of-the-year inventory of one's Christian life. More carols were sung, this time in German. A short business meeting followed with election of officers for the coming year.

*Nothing unusual about this,* one would think. But for this particular women's group it indicated an increasing maturity—a maturity in faith, knowledge, and ability. This group was larger than it had ever been before; many new faces were in the audience; the program was conducted with a definite order and was not dependent on the pastor's help.

It was only the second time in three years that we had heard a secretary's or treasurer's report. Before our arrival in Caxias do Sul the women had met four or five times a year only when a pastor came from a neighboring city. What he presented was more like a sermon than a Bible study; no one brought a Bible. Only a few owned one or saw the need for one.

The women occasionally offered teas in homes as fund-raisers. Then after the teas, the treasurer meticulously recorded their names and collected membership dues, but the group never knew how much was in their treasury because reports were never made. Only four to six women would be present for the Bible studies. The teas usually had better attendance with eight to thirty women present.

During our first year in Caxias do Sul, we met with the women once a month with four to eight women present. We sensed a need to develop leadership and create a setting for growth.

So after a year, we changed to a circle or cell system for Bible study. Six leaders were chosen, and the women of the church were divided into neighborhood groups. A week before meeting with their groups, the leaders studied with the pastor. Attendance at the monthly Bible study immediately multiplied with an average attendance of six in each circle.

All of the women were invited to the church four times a year for a general meeting for fellowship with the women of the other circles. Now, instead of recorded dues, we received freewill offerings.

How thrilled I was to hear Dona Adelina, the retiring president, conduct the December meeting. She introduced the speaker, announced the hymns, called for secretary's and treasurer's reports, and finally conducted the election. It had been necessary to write out what had to be said, and many times Dona Adelina spoke with a halting but courageous voice. It was the first year that the president of the group had been asked to participate so much in the general meetings.

Afterwards I had an opportunity to express my appreciation for her efforts during the past year. "Well, we were the first ones," she replied with an air of satisfaction, "but now that it's been started, it will be easier for the others."

And it was. Thirty years have passed, and the neighborhood Bible study circles continue to flourish. The leaders are drawn from a new generation. As time went on, the general meetings evolved into teas, which became an avenue for evangelism and fund-raising for outreach and social service projects. Women invite friends and neighbors who expect to pay an admission fee. They are popular events because of the lively programs that present topics of current interest, a variety of entertainment, singing, and the witness of the Word. Maturity has come through women discovering their gifts through biblical study and using their talents in loving service.

### RESTORED TO GOOD STANDING

A member had a daughter who was to be confirmed. The president of the congregation said it wasn't possible, however, because the family was delinquent in paying their annual church assessment. The two men were brothers; the president, a very successful butcher, and the father of the girl, a very poor subsistence farmer. An alcohol problem contributed to their poverty. The family lived in a humble, thatched-roof house that had walls of palm tree trunks stuck in the ground. The father was most grateful when I arranged for him to give a sack of soybeans to the church at harvest time in lieu of an immediate cash payment. He was thus restored to good standing so his daughter could be confirmed.

—Andrew Olsen

# Winning the Battle Over the Bottle

*James L. Peterson*

How much am I bid for this bottle of whiskey?" Ernesto* called out with exuberant anticipation. The competitive bidding began with excitement at the first big bazaar at this mission church of eighty-five persons.

Such church *festas,* or bazaars, were big money raisers for most of the established Lutheran congregations in Brazil. Those of us who were missionary pastors from the United States and Canada, working with the Brazilian Lutheran Church, were less than excited about this.

Our conviction was that Christian stewardship should be based on proportionate giving in gratitude to God and responsibility to others. The many hours and energy that were required to promote and hold a church bazaar could be better used in evangelism, Christian education, and social service.

But most of our Brazilian brothers and sisters seldom saw it that way, or if they did, still wanted bazaars. After all, they brought good folks together for a festive time. Bazaars meant easy money.

I found it hard to put a lid on such activities while I served the mission congregation in Vila Ema, a suburb in the megalopolis of São Paulo.

The congregation had geared up for its first big *festa*, offering varieties of foods and beverages, handmade doilies, embroidered towels, dresses, and other items crafted especially for their big fund-raiser. A platform had been built and tents erected. A festive air prevailed.

The day began with an outdoor worship service enhanced with the music of a visiting choir. The service went very well. The dinner tickets sold briskly. The cuisine was very international. The people enjoyed seeing me, their pastor, working as a pancake cook, frying and selling American pancakes complete with fresh fruit, whipped cream, and syrup. We also offered the traditional German potato salad with bratwursts, Brazilian-style chicken, and barbecued beef sandwiches. Beverages included Guaraná, the refreshing national soft drink, and beer.

The festival went smoothly and happily for me until Ernesto raised one of the donated items in auction—a huge bottle of whiskey. That did not please me. But to make matters worse, it was Ernesto, one of our younger men, who was the auctioneer. Ernesto was an alcoholic.

I was deeply disturbed to see this young man, with a life plagued by dependency on alcohol, swinging a big bottle of whiskey around, offering it to the highest bidder.

I prayed for patience and held my peace that Sunday afternoon. At our next church council meeting I shared my frustration and urged them not to accept that kind of donation for raising funds for the mission of Christ on earth.

To my surprise, but surely in answer to prayer, there was little opposition to my proposed ban. It was unanimous—bottles of whiskey were not to be seen at our next bazaar.

To my knowledge, Ernesto overcame his alcohol dependency. I have heard that he is now a responsible husband and father and continues to attend Alcoholics Anonymous meetings.

It was, however, more than winning the battle over the bottle; it helped focus on the deeper issues of caring for people and being responsible stewards.

---

\* The name has been changed.

# Are We Downhearted?

*Mary Jo Peterson*

*Desanimados? Não! Não! Não!"* ("Are we downhearted? No! No! No!") The Sunday school children at the Church of Hope in Ferraz de Vasconcelos sang with unrestrained gusto. As their worship leader I was pleased with their exuberance.

As we were singing the above words, I saw Senhor Clemente, the faithful custodian of our church, enter the sanctuary. Soon he was seated and singing along with us: "Troubles may come and troubles may go. I trust in Jesus come weal or woe."

*How could he help but not be downhearted?* I thought to myself. Clemente had just been diagnosed with incurable and inoperable cancer. He was in his fifties, but his remaining days of life would be few with his loving wife, three children, and a foster child.

Jim and I ministered to Clemente as his body wasted away. It was a mutual ministry, however, as he also ministered to us through his confident faith in the Lord as he lived out his last weeks of life. I can't say he never became discouraged or angry at what cancer was doing to him and his family, but I never saw or felt those emotions emanating from him. He trusted his heavenly Father to give him life after his days on this earth. He confidently entrusted his wife and children to the care of his compassionate Lord who had said, "Do not be worried and upset. . . . Believe in God and believe also in me" (John 14:1 TEV).

Clemente died, but his firm conviction of God's loving care and his witness of faith will never be forgotten by his family and friends nor by me.

He was not downhearted because he knew the God who triumphs over disease and death.

## OH, DEER ME!

Shortly after we had arrived in Campinas and enrolled in the language school, I went downtown purposely to observe Brazilians in their everyday lives and to listen to the Portuguese language as it was spoken by them. Many of the narrow streets in the bustling center had been turned into pedestrian walkways. Here people, mostly men, stood in little groups transacting business or chatting amiably.

As I strolled down the street, I noticed that men were looking at me. Some smirked, others smiled knowingly, and not a few pointed at me. I didn't think I looked all that foreign. After walking several blocks, I was feeling so uncomfortable I returned to the security of our home.

The next day I told my language teacher of the incident. After we had discussed it for some time, he asked me what I had been wearing. "Oh, nothing out of the ordinary," I explained. "These shoes and slacks and a favorite sweater."

"What kind of a sweater?" the teacher probed.

"Nothing special—a pullover, colorful, knit. On the front was the woven image of a huge buck."

After enjoying a hearty laugh, he explained that the image of *veado,* a male deer, was one of the symbols that homosexuals used to identify themselves to one another. I put the sweater away and didn't use it again until we returned to the States.

—Elden O. Landvik

# Father Is Dying!
# Can You Come?

*Robert H. Fedde*

The knock on our door sounded urgent. But their voices were even more desperate and pleading: "Father is dying! Can you come now?" The barefoot girl and her brother had arrived about 6:30 P.M. from Alvorada, deep in the virgin jungle, fifty-seven kilometers from Cascavel.

During the ride to their farm in our Volkswagen, I learned they had walked five kilometers before a truck mercifully picked them up. Our final two kilometers through the newly colonized frontier were almost impassable. Rocks and stumps damaged the bumpers and tore at the floor of our vehicle.

Finally we could drive no farther. We walked the remaining quarter mile to the doorless shack with its dirt floor. The small room was also used for storing ears of corn. In the faint glow of a single burning kerosene wick, I detected many expectant faces somberly awaiting our arrival.

A little man lay exhausted on a bed, groaning in pain. We talked together in Portuguese about Jesus Christ. He stated that he hadn't been to church for years; he didn't have a Bible. I sensed that he now sincerely wanted Jesus to forgive all his sin and desired holy communion. I sang two well-loved hymns in German, "Jesus is My Life" and "Jesus Lives." We prayed together, and he received Jesus through the bread and the wine. He appeared to rest in peace.

I bid farewell in my limited German and started the long trip back through the dark jungle, arriving home after midnight. The Lord had blessed the evening. Surely someone, somewhere had been praying, and a soul entered into the eternal presence of a loving Redeemer.

### In Christ There is Neither Rich nor Poor

In Paranavaí's workers' village, I led Bible studies in José and Maria's humble home, the only light coming from a kerosene lantern. Twenty or more people crowded into the eighteen foot by eighteen foot house of four rooms, and as many or more stood outside. We opened the house shutters, both for air circulation and so those outside could hear. When I left there, I stopped at our pediatrician's comfortable, modern home and did the same study with him and his wife. What a contrast in setting! But the Word of God applied equally to the rich as to the poor.

—Andrew Olsen

# A Rainstorm

*Mary Jo Peterson*

As I strolled over to the window of my second story hospital room in Londrina, I sensed a haunting stillness and a mysterious quiet. The sky became darker as heavy rain clouds closed in.

Then the wind began to blow, and the lovely tropical trees outside my window swayed rhythmically back and forth. I feared that the hundreds of *jabuticaba*—black fruits like super-sized bing cherries glued to the bark of the trees—would all be blown away.

A beggar woman on the street, with a large white sack over her shoulder, hastened her step. She cradled a baby in her arms. A three-year-old child toddled behind her. Students in blue and white uniforms began to run. The maid across the street scurried to gather clothes off the line and into safety while the lady of the house hurriedly closed all windows.

The wind died down as the first rains came. Finally the rain seemed to have stopped, but I heard thunderclaps and saw more ominous clouds rolling in. Soon the rain returned in pounding sheets. The unmerciful layers pelted through the trees, drenching everyone and everything caught outdoors.

At first such storms were frightening and threatening.

Rain like this had fallen every afternoon that week. Londrina was lush green after so many cleansing showers. Even the heat of the stifling March days gave way temporarily to the cool refreshment of the rains.

The storm helped me reflect on how God graciously makes the sun to shine and the rain to fall impartially on those who do good and those who do evil (Matt. 5:45). As I nestled into my hospital bed, my heart offered a prayer. "Lord, your Word is as the rain that comes down from heaven to water the earth. It provides seed for planting and food for eating. May I trust your promise that your Word will not fail to do what you plan for it in my life and the life of this beloved nation" (Isaiah 55:10,11).

# Surprised by Forgiveness

*Otto C. Tollefson*

"Frau Kuhn,* you don't know me, but I know you," the strange voice on the phone began haltingly. "I am your husband's mistress. I know you don't have children. But Erwino is the father of my two children—six-year-old Maria and Márcio, now eight."

"Why are you telling me all this?" was the only reply that Wanda Kuhn could muster.

"I am leaving him now," the stranger explained, "and moving far away to another state. Wouldn't you like to take the children and raise them as your own?"

Wanda slumped down, shocked and puzzled. She had never suspected anything. She and Erwino were in their early forties. Their marriage had been average, she thought, but childless.

When Erwino came home, she calmly told him of the phone call and that she wanted to raise those two children in their home.

I had known her only as a cousin of Frau Elena Drefahl, a wise and compassionate Christian who was mother, grandmother, and friend to everyone in the neighborhood and congregation.

Elena first told me of that phone conversation and filled me in on how her cousin, Wanda, had been a Lutheran by tradition. Elena reminded me that Wanda had attended some of our preaching missions held in the five churches in Joinville in October 1967, to

113

celebrate the four hundred fiftieth anniversary of Luther's Reformation of the Church.

Elena recalled that Wanda had responded positively to the preaching of the gospel and turned her life over to Christ. She had begun to seek ways to learn more and had sought fellowship with other believers in our weekly ECO groups that met to study, share, and pray. But Herr Kuhn had objected strenuously. He wanted his wife to stay at home and not run off to any meetings, not even Sunday morning worship.

For almost a year and a half, Wanda had respected her husband's wishes and stayed home. But to nourish her new life in Christ, she studied her Bible, read devotional books, and prayed alone in the privacy of her home.

Elena wisely suggested that it would be an appropriate time for me to visit Erwino and Wanda. I asked her to pray for this pastoral contact. I made an evening appointment. They were both cordial and friendly; the children were introduced as any other children would be and went off to bed. We chatted around the kitchen table as we drank coffee and enjoyed German kuchen.

I asked the couple if I could have a Bible reading and prayer with them before I left. Surprisingly, Erwino seemed very eager, but I wasn't sure if he was sincere or just being courteous.

I turned to chapter one of John's first epistle. After the reading, I said something like this: "John says he wrote this so that our joy may be complete. These are some of my favorite verses in the Bible. Especially verse nine, because it tells me what God does with sin that keeps me from having joy: 'If we confess our sins, God is faithful and just, and will forgive our sins, and cleanse us from all wrongdoing.'

"Let's say it's like this," I said, searching for an understandable example. "As I talk, I carelessly doodle on this tablecloth and then put my pen down. But the pen also leaks and leaves a big black blotch on this lovely, white tablecloth.

"When I notice it, I am appalled. I say to you, 'Oh, I'm so sorry. I've soiled your tablecloth.' That's like confessing my guilt.

"And you'd say, graciously, 'Oh, that's OK! Don't worry about it.' I would sense that I was forgiven. I'd be glad you weren't going to hold it against me.

"But every time friends come to visit, they'd see that ugly ink blotch. *Oh, how awful!* many would think to themselves. Your best friends might even ask, 'Which of the kids ruined your lovely tablecloth?'

"And you'd explain, 'It wasn't one of the kids; it was Pastor Otto. He was a bit careless with his pen. But that's OK.'

"And every time I would come to visit, the evidence would still be here. Once more I would feel ashamed; I would be reminded of my carelessness.

"But if you, Frau Kuhn, were to take the tablecloth, soak it in a good detergent, and wash it until the spot is removed, then the ugly blotch would be gone."

They listened attentively as I continued, "The good news from this verse is that God does forgive my sin, but it also tells me something even better: God not only forgives but cleanses me from all wrongdoing. God promises not only to forgive us but to remove the blotches in our lives."

After a few more comments and a short prayer, Erwino said quietly, "Pastor, I need to know if God will forgive me and cleanse me from all my sin.

"I have the greatest wife in the world," he said, glancing quickly at Wanda. "And I have not only been careless, I have deliberately wronged her over the years. I have lied to her thousands of times. Actually, I have lived a lie. I deceived her. I have to be honest now and tell you that she is not the mother of these children."

He poured out the story, most of which I already knew, of his mistress and the children. With tears moistening his eyes, Erwino recounted how, without his asking, Wanda had forgiven his years of adultery and had welcomed the children with genuine love.

He informed me that their friends and relatives had known of the other woman and the children, but had never told Wanda. Now they expected her to reject the children and kick the bum out. The prevailing attitude in that society was that such children were unclean. They would be judged as having dirty blood. Some expected them to be rebellious children who grow up as worthless adults, maybe even living a shameful life of sin and crime.

Erwino had already received forgiveness and acceptance from Wanda in a way that astounded all of us. Many couldn't believe it, yet I knew how she could do it. For a year and a half Wanda had walked in the light of God's Word, experiencing God's presence and forgiveness.

Wanda had also done as the apostle Peter admonished wives of unbelieving husbands (1 Peter 3:1). In a most gentle and quiet spirit, she had submitted herself to her husband so that her conduct would win him over to believe in God's Word. It had not been necessary for Wanda to say a word because Erwino saw her pure and reverent conduct.

But God who is light (1 John 1:5) now showed Erwino the darkness in which he had been living. He experienced Jesus unmasking his deceitfulness, creating harmony out of disharmony, and calling him out of darkness into light. That evening the blood of Jesus cleansed him of all sin, and Erwino began to walk in the light and to seek fellowship with other Christians.

Erwino discovered what his wife already knew: those who believe in Jesus have a joy that is complete (1 John 1:4). They worshipped together regularly. Erwino enjoyed a happy family life until his sudden death two years later. He left a son and daughter who grew up to be the pride and joy of their new mother.

---

\* Names of all persons have been changed.

# Raulino's Lucky Day

*Otto C. Tollefson*

Today was his lucky day. Raulino* rode his bike home with mounting anticipation of a great adventure. He was determined to be admired by his construction crew buddies.

His luck had actually begun the morning before when he had drawn lots with his fellow bricklayers. He won! He got first chance to try dating and seducing the attractive young woman who every day walked by their construction site. Four times a day their lustful eyes had followed her—going to work in the morning, coming home for lunch, then back to work at one o'clock, and home again late afternoon.

That same day his buddies had let Raulino eat his lunch alone in the doorway so he could flash her a smile. Again he was there to wish her an innocent *boa tarde* on her return to her job.

But this morning, on his lucky day, she had stopped for a moment to answer his question about her factory job. On her return for lunch, Raulino asked her how work had gone. After lunch he checked his watch so he would be at the faucet in front of the site, standing shirtless, washing the perspiration from his bronzed body. She had coyly observed his rippling muscles. Best of all, she accepted his invitation for a dinner date that night just to get acquainted. It was his lucky day.

His goal, however, was to impress his buddies by getting her to bed on the first date.

First, she would meet him at the park in the city square, as agreed. He knew, according to prevailing culture, she would want to date him many times before introducing him to her parents. She would ride with him on his bike under cover of early winter darkness. Dinner would be at a small restaurant on the river where Raulino was certain no one would know them.

Then he'd take her on a leisurely moonlight stroll along the river and, with luck, down to the small hotel that catered to traveling salesmen. In exchange for cash and a wink, the attendant would quickly slip him a room key without the need to register.

Raulino knew his wife would accept his excuse that his foreman needed him to meet with a client to go over details of a possible construction. She'd have dinner alone with their five children.

After shaving and showering, Raulino reached up high to the top of the armoire to get a folded shirt. As he pulled the shirt, some old magazines and brochures fell to the floor. Bending to pick them up, his eyes caught the top pamphlet, "The Cry of the Unwanted Child," and the accompanying photo of a young child with sad and haunting eyes.

Later that week Raulino came to my office for his weekly preparation for leading his small fellowship group. Coincidentally, the theme was temptation. He penitently told me in detail of his temptation and schemes.

"Pastor, I just couldn't do it." Raulino confessed. "In that moment I knew that my sin would bring suffering to the girl and maybe produce an unwanted child. God had confronted me by that brochure I had read so many years before. It's written as though the words are those of a child conceived in lust instead of love.

"I knew my wonderful wife was getting supper for our children. They were all wanted and loved by us.

"God had confronted me. I remembered how Joseph had resisted Potiphar's wife and said, 'How could I do such an immoral thing and sin against God?'" (Genesis 39:9 TEV).

Raulino recounted how the next day as he biked to work he had prayed for courage to explain to his buddies—anxious for details of the date—what, by God's grace, had happened.

He admitted to them that from the beginning he knew it was wrong, yet he had willingly embraced the temptation. He showed them the brochure God had used to confront him.

Some respected him; others thought he had thrown away an opportunity to show how macho he really was. They knew Raulino had now ruined their chances of ever having a lucky day with her.

That evening as we studied together, two scripture texts came alive as Raulino related them to his life. First, "A person is tempted when he is drawn away and trapped by his own evil desire" (James 1:14 TEV).

Second, "Every test that you have experienced is the kind that normally comes to people. But God keeps his promise, and he will not allow you to be tested beyond your power to remain firm; at the time you are put to the test, he will give you strength to endure it, and so provide you with a way out" (1 Corinthians 10:13 TEV).

Raulino's blue eyes lit up. "God did provide me a way out," he said. "God was faithful even when I was bent on being unfaithful. It really was my lucky day."

---

* The name has been changed.

# Return to the Asphalt Jungle

*Robert H. Fedde*

Emerson,* a seventeen-year-old marijuana addict, was one of thirty-eight Lutheran youth from Rio de Janeiro participating in a full week of confirmation instruction at the mountain retreat center at Araras. His parents were inactive members who lived near the beautiful Ipanema beach. After morning studies led by their three pastors, the youth enthusiastically participated in sports, swimming, and hikes. The evening was a time for biblical learning through viewing filmstrips and for spirited singing accompanied by guitars. Emerson was one of the guitar players and easily picked up several new youth songs.

On Friday, our last night together, we gathered around a bonfire for a time of reflection and prayer. Several openly shared how the week had challenged and changed them. Emerson related how the week had helped him, and that he now felt he belonged to a new family. We closed by joining hands, forming a large circle around the fire, offering prayers of thanksgiving for the week, and interceding for each other on our return to the asphalt jungle.

The following Sunday afternoon Emerson took his guitar on a witnessing visit to his marijuana gang. Presumedly because of his treason, Emerson was shot twice by a gang member, once through the liver. The prognosis was that he would not live. Many rallied around him in prayer, and Emerson recovered. Our prayers were that Emerson would not only live, but that he would meet Jesus in a more intimate way as his ever present Lord and Savior.

### For Whom the Tune Tolls

When Dorothy and I arrived in Campinas for language study, we worshiped with the local Lutheran congregation. The services alternated between the German and Portuguese languages. When a death occurred, however, the bereaved gathered at the next Sunday service. Then when the death was announced, it was the custom that the choir sang for the bereaved a traditional hymn of consolation and of thanksgiving for the life of the deceased. The usual selection was the German hymn, "Wo findet die Seele die Heimat, die Ruhe?", which roughly translated asks, "Where does the soul find its resting place?"

Dorothy did not understand the words, but the melody was the same tune as "Home, Sweet Home." As the choir sang, Dorothy, with fond memories of home, broke down and wept. The congregation, unaware of the meaning of the melody, assumed that she was one of the bereaved. As the members filed out of the church, they stopped to give her their condolences. This happened a number of times until Dorothy was accustomed to the practice.

—Richard Wangen

---

*The name has been changed.

# God Walked With Them

*Otto C. Tollefson*

Karin Brümüller was a sad and bitter person when she arrived at a Lutheran Marriage Encounter weekend with her husband, Ottokar. They did not realize how profound changes would begin to heal their lives and marriage.

Looking back, Karin reflected, "I didn't even think that I could change. I was preoccupied with myself and our marriage, but I felt helpless to do anything about it. I needed something profound to take away my depression, which seemed to have no end."

This was not the Karin I had first known twenty years before. She and Ottokar were serious but exuberant teenagers when we arrived in Joinville, Santa Catarina, in 1965. Both attended our church youth groups; Karin sang in the youth choir directed by my wife, Barbara. They had been married for fifteen years when they accepted an invitation to a Lutheran Marriage Encounter weekend in June 1985.

Karin recalled that a change began in her when a speaker stated, "God does not make junk." She finally understood why she had considered herself to be nothing but garbage.

Some years before, while doing housework, Karin had suffered a strong shock from the electric oven. She was six months pregnant at the time. Soon afterwards, while traveling to a distant city, their second daughter was born prematurely and lived for only forty hours.

Karin blamed herself; she judged she had failed both as a mother and as a wife. She didn't believe that God, much less her husband and daughter, could ever forgive her. She meekly resigned herself to any difficulty, accepting it as punishment for not being more careful. Hiding her anguish and loneliness, she presented herself to others as a strong, capable woman.

Karin had always worked hard, but now she compulsively worked more than necessary. As she did her housework, her mind accused her, *You deserve to suffer. You are worthless.* A great emptiness persisted even after God presented them with a son, Rudyard.

For many years Ottokar had sensed he was living with a Karin different from the one he had married. Now she was serious and closed, always busy, looking for even more work.

He remembered, "She no longer had time for me. She smiled very little, and her zest for life was gone. I didn't understand what had happened, and I never could imagine what was going on in her head or in her heart. I knew she was sad over the loss of our child, but I was not aware of her self-rejection. I asked myself, *What is wrong? Am I not capable of making her happy?*

"But," he confessed, "I wasn't happy either. I too felt the loss of our baby and tried to be understanding of Karin, but nothing helped. Our marriage was threatened; I thought she maybe didn't love me any more."

During their Marriage Encounter weekend they both began to share their feelings. It was not until a year later, however, when they attended a second weekend that Karin could talk openly about her self-recrimination and guilt feelings. Ottokar saw a great change slowly unfold in her; she became more confident and vivacious.

Karin explained, "When I discovered that God loved me and I was not junk, and that what had happened was a misfortune and not a judgment on me, I felt myself once again accepted by God. The biggest weight of my life had been lifted. Only then did I see clearly that God had faithfully been by our side the whole time."

She remembered how a few days before the premature birth and death of their baby, she had been at a women's meeting where the theme was "The Lord is my shepherd, I have everything I need" (Psalm 23:1 TEV).

The baby's burial had taken place five hundred miles from home in a small city where they had lived when they were first married. The local pastor used the same verse from Psalm 23 for their comfort. On their return to Joinville, this psalm was again used at the baby's memorial service.

Just a coincidence? Karin now confidently answers no. She tells how years later, at their son's confirmation, when the pastor called the boy next in line, just ahead of Rudyard, to come forward for the blessing, he gave him Psalm 23:1 as the theme for his life.

Karin thought that God could certainly have confirmed his forgiveness of her by having this verse given to her son. Then to her great surprise, the same verse was repeated, which hadn't happened before. Rudyard also received Psalm 23:1 as his verse for life! The emotional impact on her was so great that she started to cry. No one knew why, but she knew. "God had spoken to me and shown me how much he loves me," she says. "Like a Shepherd, God had walked with us."

By the end of their second Marriage Encounter weekend, Karin had been ready to give talks on weekends for couples. Ottokar, however, thought this would never be possible judging that they had nothing to say that would be helpful to others. Instead, they served as a support couple, doing behind-the-scenes tasks. But Karin continually pointed out to Ottokar how important God had been in their life and how other couples might be facing conflicts similar to theirs. Gradually Ottokar began to see that they were not being the light in the world that they could be.

They have made themselves available, through the work of Lutheran Marriage Encounter, to love their neighbor as they have been loved by God. Besides participating actively in St. Matthew's parish in Joinville, they give leadership to Lutheran Marriage Encounter as the co-executive lay couple for the South American region.

Ottokar says, "Marriage Encounter still seems to be the most effective way for us to help a couple develop a good relationship with themselves as well as with God."

His hope is that others won't be as hard on themselves and as insensitive as they were. Ottokar says:

> We want others to know it isn't necessary to wait until God becomes as insistent as he had been with us.
>
> There are times in our lives when we feel God very close to us. Those are very special and unforgettable moments. They change our lives and our priorities; they renew our faith and make our relationship with God much more intimate. We recognize his great love and power. We sense that God is concerned about us and was always by our side, even if we often did not realize it.

Ottokar and Karin have accepted a ministry to encourage other couples to join them on a journey of love, assured that God truly walks with them.

# Freed from Terror

*Ruth Kasperson*

Terror struck me like lightning when I heard distant voices of men singing in a staccato fashion. Their voices became increasingly louder and more distinct as they approached our mission clearing at the jungle's edge. Their chant announced that they had come to plunder, rape, and steal.

I was alone with our three small children on that stifling hot summer night. My husband, Bob, was away on a trip. The children were finally asleep, and I had been trying to sleep when those voices jarred me awake.

We had heard that a band of men were encamped deeper into the jungle. They were convicts from prisons in the neighboring states, released to land companies that employed them to clear the jungle for development in north Paraná.

By day these released convicts were busy chopping down trees, but occasionally at night they ventured into Cianorte, the new frontier town. On their arrival, citizens cleared the streets and locked themselves behind closed doors.

But I had no doors to lock! I was paralyzed with fear as I realized how totally vulnerable we were. Our mission residence was still under construction and had open doorways and windows facing toward the very path on which the terrorists were fast approaching. There were no neighbors for many blocks. Phones were nonexistent.

My trembling hands reached for a flashlight and Bible. I hurried into a room less visible to the road and crouched behind an overstuffed chair. By this time my whole body was shaking. With difficulty I pressed the flashlight's button and prayed silently as I opened my Bible, *Lord Jesus, be with us and give me the words you have for me.*

I began reading Psalm 3. I was arrested by the words, "I cry aloud to the Lord, and he answers me. . . . I lie down and sleep; I wake again, for the Lord sustains me" (vv. 4,5 NRSV). I read further, but those words reverberated in my mind and heart. I realized that was God's message for me. A calmness embraced me, and God's peace descended upon my heart and mind.

The voices of the men faded in the distance. I came out from my hiding place, tumbled into bed, and slept soundly until morning. God's Word had driven out the terror caused by the convicts' chanted words.

Whenever I recall that experience, I am reminded how the Word has power to sustain us every moment of our lives.

## CAN'T ARGUE WITH QUICK AND EASY

Our domestic help, or maids, who came to us fresh from the farms often proved to be a great challenge. Their way of doing things often differed from ours.

This became apparent the day I heard a resounding thud coming from the kitchen. I hurried in to see the maid standing in a puddle of water and poised to throw another bucket full of water into the emptied refrigerator. The exploding splash drenched us both and splattered throughout the kitchen. She then reached for a broom and swept the water out the door. That done, she turned and asked me, "What could be quicker and easier than that?"

—Ruth Kasperson

# A Norwegian Angel Said, "Fear Not"

*Barbara J. Tollefson*

During his senior year in college, my husband, Otto, had been drawn to the World Mission Prayer League's new work in Brazil. His enthusiasm captured my interest, and we read everything there was about the mission. After speaking with Verne Lavik, a member of his congregation who had visited the site of this pioneer work in north Paraná, we had a fair idea of what life in interior Brazil would be like.

We experienced very little culture shock in 1958 when we arrived in beautiful, modern Campinas for a year of language and orientation studies.

No culture shock except for the public meat market! We enjoyed going to the neighborhood street market and the downtown public market. Our shopping bags bulged with exotic tropical fruits and fresh vegetables. But the meat market literally left me ill.

There was no cold storage for the meat. Trucks pulled up to the market loaded with meat that had been slaughtered on the same or the previous day. Men with hooded cloaks over their heads and backs carried sides of beef or pork stuck to meat hooks. After transporting several such slabs of meat to and from the trucks, the once white robes were deeply stained and filthy dirty.

I could get past that sight, but not the swarms of flies on the meat that hung in the open for extended periods in hot weather. For many weeks our family was vegetarian, except for cold cuts and, occasionally, canned meat.

I decided I must overcome my fear of contaminated meat. So I bravely set off to the market with written instructions in hand in case the butcher couldn't understand my faulty Portuguese.

I had repeated to myself, over and over, *um meio kilo de concho mole, por favor*—a half kilo of beef filet, please. But once at the counter, the words stuck in my throat. I could not order. I moved to the back of the line and watched others easily place their orders.

Then a hand touched my shoulder, and a sweet voice said, "Why, Barbara, how nice to see you. How are you doing?" It was Mary, an elegant Norwegian lady whose husband was an industrialist in Campinas. She had invited several of the pastors' wives to her lovely home and had been so friendly and helpful to us who had recently arrived in Brazil.

I poured out my story, embarrassed that I could not buy that meat on which all those horrible, dirty, disease-carrying flies had settled.

She quietly assured me, "Oh, Barbara! You need to see the beautiful things about Brazil—the spectacular vegetation and marvelous fruits. The wonderful sun. You'll take the meat home, and you will rinse it before baking it in the oven for a long time. Don't be afraid. It won't hurt you or your family. It will make a lovely dinner."

She held out her hand. "Let me help you order it."

Through this Norwegian angel, God had provided the nudge that I needed.

# Doní, Our Brazilian Daughter

*Ray Holter*

Our parish youth group elected Doní Wendt to be president because she was a good dancer. Little did her peers know the impact Doní would have on their program and lives. She also would become the one we lovingly called our Brazilian daughter.

This teenager was the middle of eight children growing up on a poor farm near the village of Salto do Jacuí, Rio Grande do Sul.

Her father was uneducated but very wise. It may have been his sense of inadequacy of the education given in the village school that led him to regularly line up his eight children to direct questions to them. He made each one think through the responses and not just parrot back answers. These exercises in reasoning prepared Doní to be a brilliant teacher in the public school system. This, together with her participation in the youth group, helped Doní develop her natural leadership qualities.

Doní's life changed when she attended our first youth retreat. We were reading through the Gospel of John. On the second day, she informed me that she and the other girls wanted to experience what John 1:12 promised—becoming children of God through receiving Jesus in their lives. Her focus and goals in life changed through this relationship.

Because of the great distance from her home to Cruz Alta where we lived, we invited Doní to live with us during the three years she attended college. Later, when we served in Rio Negro, Paraná, she also lived with us while she worked as a teacher and school supervisor.

At a gathering of the Lutheran pastors of our district, Doní challenged them to make youth ministry a higher priority. To her, the pastors had appeared unconcerned. We were surprised how they, in that macho society, graciously accepted her perceptive evaluation. In the following years we saw evidence of effective youth ministry in more parishes.

Even though Doní was Lutheran, the Catholic sisters invited her to teach the religion courses in the Roman Catholic school.

Just before we closed out our ten year ministry in Brazil, I had the privilege of presiding at Doní's marriage to Hildo Zuege, a member of the Cruz Alta youth group.

Tragedy cut short their happy marriage, however. Doní died at age thirty-two while giving birth to their first child, Demaris Doní. We received a letter and picture of Demaris on the occasion of her confirmation in the faith. We perceived that she was following in the footsteps of the mother she never knew.

At one time we counted fourteen young people who had entered or were preparing for part- or full-time Christian service as pastors or teachers, or in other leadership roles in the church. Doní had been directly or indirectly instrumental in their hearing the call to service.

The seed had fallen on good soil. It brought forth fruit in her life and in many with whom she so joyfully shared the promise of new life in Christ.


### Eggsactly

Before supermarkets were introduced, customers stood behind counters and asked for groceries, item by item. Jack Aamot, newly arrived in Brazil, wished to buy a dozen eggs but lacked the vocabulary. Much to the enjoyment of the other shoppers, Jack flashed twelve fingers, put his thumbs in his armpits and then cackled loudly as he waved his arms up and down.

# Jesus Gave Him Peace

*Robert Roiko*

My wife, Alona, and I were having a peaceful review of our busy Sunday when an unexpected knock on the front door interrupted our conversation. A tall, young man stood at the entrance. "My name is Armindo Schulz,* and I need to speak to you," he said directly. A troubled expression blanketed his face.

We invited him into our living room. For the next hour, Armindo poured out his personal struggles. "I can't seem to find peace. I am very nervous," he explained. We learned that he had been in the military and was now a dentist in the downtown area of a large metropolis. His business was thriving, but lately he had been finding it difficult to hold his dental instruments without dropping them. He had attended several spiritualist meetings, but his agitation only seemed to be getting worse.

Armindo's fiancee, Maria, a member of our church, had suggested that he visit her pastor. Alona and I listened, and then we offered to pray with Armindo, asking God for peace and direction in his life. We shared Jesus' promise, "Peace I leave with you; my peace I give to you. I do not give to you as the world gives. Do not let your hearts be troubled, and do not let them be afraid" (John 14:27 NRSV).

As he was leaving, Armindo asked to borrow some Christian reading material that might help him. The next day I went to his office and gave him a Christian book of devotional and Bible readings on how to deal with daily anxieties.

Shortly afterwards, Armindo and Maria attended church. Following the services a smiling Armindo embraced me. "Pastor, I have given my cares over to the Lord. I am so happy. The Bible verses on peace with God have given me a new direction. Thank you so much."

Later Armindo and Maria were married, and Armindo became a strong witness for Christ not only in the church but among his business acquaintances. Both Maria and Armindo had a serene spirit about them that was very powerful.

Tragically, a few years later, Armindo and his uncle were killed instantly in a car accident. At the funeral, Maria spoke of her husband's strong faith in the resurrected Lord.

Armindo and Maria had received the peace Jesus gives and joyously shared it with all whom they knew.

---

\* The names have been changed.

## Part Three

# God Loves the One
# Who Gives Gladly

# In the Community of Suffering

*Otto C. Tollefson*

Among our Brazilian sisters and brothers there are many role models of suffering and great generosity. Herr and Frau Zwetsch are one couple worth imitating.

They had moved to the coastal industrial city of Joinville with their five children in hope of enjoying a life better than they had in the interior on a nonproductive farm. Herr Zwetsch traded the security of family and friends for earning a minimum wage as an unskilled laborer. They rented a shack in an area that was a step above a slum. She kept her house clean and attractive.

Frau Zwetsch asked my permission, as her new pastor, to gather the neighborhood children on Saturday mornings to teach them a Bible story and hymn. She had one little, old-fashioned, black and white Bible storybook and a dog-eared paperback collection of hymns. We were able to provide her more colorful and up-to-date teaching material.

Every Saturday she gathered children into a living room that could not have measured more than eight feet square. Her furnishings consisted of one small square table pushed into the corner and a few rough benches.

Within a year the Zwetsch family was looking for a house to buy. They had two requirements: First, it had to be in the same general area so she could continue her mission to the children. Second, the living room had to be large enough to hold her growing children's Bible club. She always examined one room first—not the kitchen nor the bedrooms but the living room.

One day I brought her a box of clothes that our five children had outgrown. I was amazed when she told me how the week before she had gathered some of her kitchen utensils and a bundle of clothes from her family to give to a family whose husband was now working with Herr Zwetsch.

"They have just moved here from the interior like we did. They are such a poor family," she said. "We will share with them what you have brought us."

The Zwetsch family belonged to what Albert Schweitzer, the renown medical missionary to Africa, called "the fellowship of those who bear the mark of pain."

Schweitzer cautioned that those who have been delivered from pain must not think they are now free again and at liberty to take up life as it was before, entirely forgetful of the past. But rather, now that their eyes are open with regard to pain and anguish, they must bring others to experience the deliverance they have enjoyed.

The Zwetsch family had suffered and were a part of the community of suffering. Like the Macedonian Christians, who the apostle Paul says are worth imitating (2 Corinthians 8:2), they had been severely tested by the troubles they went through, but their joy was so great. They were extremely generous in their giving even though they were very poor.

# Choking Out Stewardship

*Robert H. Fedde*

Lies, threats of murder, retaliation, and physical assault were not what I expected when I led my parish into a new method of financial support.

The century-old system for the Lutheran congregations in Brazil had been a standardized annual assessment on each family. This could be contributed monthly, quarterly, or annually. Some parishes had church dues collectors; others required contributions to be brought to the church office or handed to the treasurer. Offerings were not a part of the liturgical worship.

The payment of the assessment was enforced by denying baptisms, confirmations, weddings, and funerals to those who were not current with their financial obligations. Many families scrambled to catch up several years of overdue payments before the pastoral act would be performed. A common byproduct was resentment toward the clergy and church.

The two largest congregations in our parish, Terra Roxa* and Rio Branco,* decided to implement a new stewardship program created by missionary Pastor Milton Olson and launched by him with great success in a number of congregations.

But what seemed to us American and Canadian missionaries as a natural, evangelical approach to stewardship was a paradigm shift for traditional Brazilian Lutherans.

Now each confirmed member or family unit would be invited, as a response to God's grace, to contribute to the church in proportion to how the Lord blessed them financially. They were encouraged to pledge annually, preferably a percentage of their income, and to make the offering a part of their worship experience.

We carefully prepared the soil, educationally and spiritually. We introduced the program after a week of evangelism led by Brazilian evangelist Newton P. Beyer. All went well. The spirituality of the congregations increased together with the monetary contributions.

Where the Lord builds his temple, however, Satan pitches his tent. Perhaps it was the new enthusiasm for mission and ministry that at first blinded us to the thorn bushes threatening the young seedlings.

"This stewardship business is a trick of the pastors to get people to worship services," some complained.

In the Rio Branco congregation, former church council members met secretly and opposed the new stewardship program. They spread lies that the congregation was trying to obtain all the members' assets, farms, and homes. In retaliation, the new church council voted to expel from the congregation those who were opposing the program. This caused a serious rift in the congregation.

The former president threatened to kill all the members of the new church council. One night at the local bar, he grabbed a quart beer bottle and bashed one of the new council members over the head, breaking the bottle and knocking him out. The ex-president then jumped from the table, grasped the bottle by the neck and, with the jagged edges, poked it several times into the face of the unconscious man. The victim was rushed to the hospital where doctors attempted to repair the lacerated face.

Unfortunately, as time went by, the opposition to the new stewardship approach won out. The congregation retreated to the traditional system of assessing dues and sponsoring church *festas* where revenue from barbecued dinners, gambling, and drinking would help finance the church's mission. It was evident that some seeds had fallen among the thorn bushes, which grew up and choked the plants.

---

\* The names of congregations have been changed.

# Guinea Pigs and Collectors, Steaks and Beer

*Elden O. Landvik*

How should a congregation fund their mission and ministry? When I arrived to serve the parish in Taquara, I was not prepared for their methods of raising money. To my dismay four Portuguese words—*coelhinho, cobrador, churrasco, chope*—seemed to answer this question for them and other traditional Lutheran congregations.

A popular method was their weekend *festas,* or fund-raising celebrations, held in a sprawling building that had been constructed for these semiannual events. A large room had been set aside for the sole purpose of grilling *churrascos,* barbecued T-bone steaks, chicken, and pork. Much of the *festa* income was derived from selling delicious dinners.

*Festas* also featured gambling. Besides the roulette wheels, they had invented a rather ingenious game of chance. An elevated, octagonal platform had been constructed, which measured roughly fifteen feet across. All around, on the outer edge of the platform, little wooden houses were placed so that the openings, which served as doors, faced toward the center of the platform. These were all numbered, except for one, on the top of which was a small cross. This represented the church.

After bets were placed, a *coelhinho,* guinea pig, would be let loose in the center of the platform. If it went into the little house on which a man had placed his bet, he would win that round. If the *coelhinho* scurried into the house with the cross on it, the parish would get the money.

The real measure of the success of these *festas*, however, was the number of kegs of *chope,* beer, that were sold.

The second method of financial support was not offerings received at worship services but the billing of members for their annual dues. The church council decided what each family should pay, based on the national church's recommendation. In this congregation a *cobrador,* or collector, then tried to collect what each family had been assessed. For this service he was paid ten percent of whatever he was able to collect. The cobrador was not a popular man. Many members hid when they saw him coming or made excuses for not being able to pay.

After I had presented several sessions on the biblical and evangelical principles of stewardship to the church council, they reluctantly agreed to discontinue the practice and instead let the people themselves pledge what they wanted to give. Why would people give if they didn't have to? The result, to the amazement of the council, was that income rose substantially.

It is impossible to know for how many this was a response to the gospel. Perhaps many were just happy to have the church council off their backs. At least the people had been set free to give of their own free will.

It was my hope that some of them would come to realize that our giving should be a grateful response to our gift-giving God and never a matter of law.

# A New Temple Is Built

*Fayette Massingill*

It took about ten years, but finally the beautiful building was completed, providing a place where the believers could gather for worship and fellowship. It was more than a building—it was a witness to the joyful reception of the gospel by the people of Mafra.

The parish of Rio Negro had been established in the late nineteenth century. In the early 1960s, the parish decided to add another congregation to better serve the growing membership. The location would be in the city of Mafra, across the river that separates the states of Santa Catarina and Paraná. First they erected a wooden building for worshiping. After the permanent sanctuary was built, this temporary one would become the social hall.

Because of runaway inflation and escalating monthly interest rates, building loans were not even considered. In such an economy, a building fund would only lose purchasing power. The alternative was to purchase building supplies immediately as the money was contributed until there would be sufficient material to begin construction.

Although permanent buildings were stucco-covered brick, lumber was still needed for framing, rafters, and interior work. It was my privilege to go to the forest with the men of the congregation to cut trees; the logs were then hauled to the mill where they would be traded for lumber. It was reminiscent of the pioneer days in the United States.

It was truly heartwarming to see the Holy Spirit at work, creating joy and fellowship as the people worked together to accumulate materials and construct a building. The laborers were all volunteers except for the foreman.

There was continual prayer as the building went up in stages. We held special times of celebration and reflection on God's Word after each stage. The two most special events were the completion of the roof and the dedication of the completed building. I was there for the roof celebration. My successor, Pastor Ray Holter, was there for the joyous, final dedication.

During the whole process I was constantly reminded of the early church: "Now the whole group of those who believed were of one heart and soul" (Acts 4:32 NRSV). But most important was the witness this group made to the whole community and to the Evangelical Church of the Lutheran Confession in Brazil.

There is nothing more beautiful or inspiring than witnessing people receiving the gospel and sharing it with others. These are the memories that make living a joy.

BAREFOOT IN PARADISE

It is reported that John Abel, at the groundbreaking for the new school in Cianorte, reflected on how they were among the first to settle in that new frontier town in the middle of the jungle. Instead of saying they had arrived without resources, *sem meios,* John stated they had arrived *sem meias,* without socks.

# God Provides

*Charles D. Eidum*

When I was asked how many beds were in the Evangelical Hospital in Ponta Grossa, I could honestly state there were sixty—but they were all in a storage room. And we had no plan to change that.

For seventeen years our Evangelical Society, a subsidiary of the Good Shepherd Lutheran Church in Ponta Grossa, Parana, had worked to get to this point—owners of a nonfunctioning hospital.

God had blessed the society's vision and labors to this point. We could proudly say that the basement level of the facility housed the important work of examining women for breast cancer. But the rest of the hospital was empty.

One day I invited Manfred Renner,* the president, and Ivo Fischer, treasurer of the hospital's board of trustees, to have lunch with me. I laid before them a double challenge. First, to hire a hospital administrator; second, to open the hospital by the time we celebrated our eighteenth anniversary as the Evangelical Society.

The men logically protested that the hospital did not have the funds for the salary of a good administrator.

"Hire the right administrator," I said, "and he will not only raise enough money to pay for his own salary, but he will be the key to opening the hospital by our anniversary."

They accepted the challenge and hired an administrator.

The trustees then wrestled with ways to raise more money. The most attractive idea was to hold a lottery with big items, such as a car, TV, and refrigerator, as prizes.

One member cited the impressive track record of other organizations that had used lotteries. They proved that with consistent, hard work, lotteries can raise substantial sums of money. He promised that our lottery could bring in a specific amount—what we needed to open the hospital.

I reminded them that they had chosen the name *Evangelical* Hospital. A lottery would be totally contrary to the message we wanted to give their city. The board reluctantly accepted what I said, at least for that night.

In less than two months, I received an urgent phone call from Manfred, asking if I could come to the hospital for a short meeting. As president, he wanted as many members of the board together as possible. Representatives of a local company were coming to present the hospital with a monetary gift. He didn't know the amount, but he wanted others there with him to receive the gift.

We gave the guests a tour of the empty facilities and then adjourned to the boardroom. After a short ceremony the head of the company's delegation handed an envelope to Manfred, our capable leader and expressive speaker. When he opened the envelope and saw the amount of the check, he gave one word—the exuberant exclamation, *"Puxa!"* Wow! I know he would have said that no matter what the amount. Manfred always honors all givers for any size gift.

Without saying anything further, he handed the check to me. The check was for the exact amount promised by the board member if the hospital had done the lottery. We experienced again that God has his ways. God provides!

The Evangelical Hospital opened within its one year goal. Its ministry initially was only to pregnant women, many without means to pay for medical services. We also initiated a chaplaincy program.

Now many people have an opportunity to hear the evangel— the good news—in an Evangelical Hospital.

---

*The names have been changed.

# The Grace of Giving

*Ruth Holter*

I was disturbed the first time I saw elderly Ivo Stein* and his young wife, Maria, with a toddler and an infant in arms. *It should not be this way,* I thought. *Having babies is for young people. These children will most likely grow up not having a father.* Among the rural poor there are few jobs for women and no life insurance or welfare assistance.

They had come to have their second child baptized in a very humble building that served as the church in Vila Nova. Thirty to forty others, mostly of German descent, were in attendance, most of them equally as poor.

These peasants worked small plots of land and raised a few chickens. Only the more affluent owned a cow. The houses were nondescript, of single wall construction with red tile roofs. Shutters covered the openings made for light and ventilation. Such windows weren't really needed for ventilation because of the many cracks in the boards. Some houses had wood floors; many were dirt.

Cooking was done on wood cook stoves, and water was pulled from wells. A few had the luxury of an outdoor water pump. Most families were clean and appeared content.

The age difference between Ivo, at least sixty-five years old, and very young Maria caught my attention at the baptism. We did not see them again until they came for the baptism of their third child.

This concern led me to become acquainted with this old-young family. It was unusual to have *Frau Farrer,* Mrs. Pastor, as I was known, visit in these rural homes far from the city church. Initially I would be met with a reserved, questioning attitude.

It was that way with Ivo and Maria. But after a number of visits, I discovered that Ivo was truly a man with a father's heart and love.

He confided that he wanted to be more active in church but was uncomfortable because of the system of taxation or church dues. The councils in most of the traditional churches showed no partiality for rich or poor. All were required to contribute the same amount. Those who were not current in their annual assessment would be denied baptism of their babies or other pastoral services.

Ivo explained how difficult it was for him to provide for his family and meet this financial obligation.

I had the of joy of explaining to him that in our parish we had recently introduced a stewardship program that was based on God's grace and our response of gratitude, according to our ability to contribute.

"You mean for as little two *centavos* (less than a penny), I can be considered a faithful member?" he asked.

I assured him that his participation in worship and congregational life was most important, independent of the size of his contribution. Once the law was removed, Ivo became faithful in worship and contributed out of love.

We were not able to provide him life insurance or guarantee his family any social welfare program. But the Steins did discover a caring family among God's people.

---

* The names have been changed.

# The Man Called Peter

*Robert Maland*

A few weeks after arriving in Marília, São Paulo, in September 1959, to open mission work, I heard about Dr. Peter Wirth, a Protestant rancher, who didn't belong to any church in the area. Recently he had been nearly killed when his vehicle was struck by a train. I learned that his father had been a pioneer from Switzerland in 1898 and had acquired extensive landholdings. The father had died, leaving his son, Peter, to head the original Paredão Ranch of 30,000 acres of cotton, coffee, cattle, and sugar cane—plus seventeen other farms and ranches scattered in two states. I had been told that about 500 Brazilian workers and their families—a whole village—lived on Dr. Pedro's Paredão Ranch. It would be easy to imagine that he might be one of the richest men in the area. He had some Protestant background, but would he consider worshiping with us?

My wife, Ann, and I had started our evangelism by knocking on doors and following leads. We included the Wirth family in our prayers for God's guidance on follow-up. The time came when I felt the Spirit was prompting me to have the courage to drive to Paredão Ranch, twenty miles out of town, for an initial contact with the Wirths. Almost forty years later, I can still vividly recall my apprehension as I drove down the driveway lined with tall, majestic palm trees. Would I be ordered off the premises? "Lord,"

I prayed, "prepare the hearts and minds of this family that my good intentions will not be rejected."

I introduced myself to Dr. Pedro and his wife, Margo, and told how we had come from the United States, and after studying Portuguese for a year, we were appointed to begin a Lutheran ministry in Marília. They no doubt perceived that with my accent and limited vocabulary, I had plenty of room for improvement.

They graciously listened as I told them we had found a home in Marília for only sixty dollars per month, if we would do the remodeling and painting. I described a long, narrow building, separate from the house, with four rooms in a row. We were planning to use them for Sunday school. There was also a thirty foot by thirty foot lean-to extending from the back of the house. This covered area with its ceramic flooring could seat sixty to eighty persons for worship.

Dr. Pedro and his family seemed interested when I explained that we were planning to have our first service in two weeks.

A week later, Dr. Pedro, Margo, and their four children arrived to look over our new site. They indicated that they not only wanted to worship with us but would furnish transportation for others on the ranch to come to the services. Three other families working for him also had Swiss Protestant backgrounds. They were our partners in evangelism before we had our first service!

Two other Swiss families joined the Wirths for the first service, together with others we had invited by word of mouth and by our daily, five minute radio broadcast.

The Word of God was finding receptive hearts. By Christmas, Margo, an accomplished musician, had offered to play our old, upright piano. I had equipped it with heavy duty rubber rollers so we could roll it out of the living room for each service in our backyard temple.

In spite of the heaviest sustained rain that I've experienced in my life, sixty-four persons attended our Christmas service. Besides accompanying the Sunday school children and congregation for Christmas songs, Margo also played for her son Marcos' violin rendition. It was truly a time of celebration.

Dr. Pedro and Jacob, a Swiss mechanic and machinist, who with his wife had also become members of our congregation, headed the team for finding land for a new church. The site chosen was in a growing residential part of Marília.

Several Sundays later we had groundbreaking ceremonies with youth and adults shoveling dirt from the corner double lot. All the members were committed to doing what they could to bring about the construction of the building. Dr. Pedro offered his draftsman out at the ranch to draw up plans for the new church and also his construction team for the building phase. It was a missionary's dream come true—to have capable members sharing in the responsibilities.

Dr. Pedro and Margo had a growing missionary concern. Among other projects, this Swiss family quietly sponsored Toshiko Arai, a Japanese Lutheran woman, to come to Brazil to help in evangelism among the Japanese families where our mission was present. Dr. Pedro wrote a substantial check to Ken and Carola Stenberg when he learned they had taken money from their household funds to pay for Toshiko's unexpected customs charges on entering Brazil. As her sponsors, the Wirths wanted to assume that responsibility.

The Wirths also helped make it possible for Carlos to follow his dream of further education and service in the church. (See "Whatever Happened to Carlos?", page 163.)

Later, under the ministries of our successors, Gaylord and Gloria Grant and Eugene and Lorraine Foehringer, Dr. Pedro assumed regional church responsibilities in both the states of São Paulo and Paraná.

A missionary colleague told me how he showed American congregations a slide of a group of men conversing at the first gathering of lay leaders from our mission congregations. He mentioned that most were semiliterate laborers or sharecroppers; one had the equivalent of a high school education. Then he asked, "Which one is the Swiss millionaire with a doctorate in agronomy?" Dr. Pedro's clothes, body language, and speech were such that he blended in with the people he so loved, respected, and served.

That fine service came to a sudden end on December 18, 1975 when a big truck crashed into Dr. Pedro's car and killed him. God had graciously brought him and his family into our lives. Like Abraham of old, he was blessed to be a blessing, and he truly blessed the lives of many.

## No More Cart Rides

In September 1959, Ruth and I, fresh out of language school, arrived to begin mission work in Paranavaí. We were enthralled with the cute, two-wheeled horse-drawn carts parked in front of the post office, with their drivers waiting for customers. We thought it would be an excellent way to see the town and savor its frontier flavor. Although the driver seemed surprised at our request, he agreed to drive us around town. There weren't any tourist spots, but we enjoyed the rustic feel of the frontier—no asphalt, just dirt and clutter, horses and jeeps.

We did stop to meet the Presbyterian pastor in his home, however. I left Ruth in the cart as I went to knock on the door. The pastor came out, and we visited for a bit. He seemed friendly until I pointed out my blonde wife sitting in the cart. He got very nervous, gave a quick excuse, and abruptly went into the house, leaving me standing on the porch. I returned to the cart, and we finished the tour.

It didn't take many days before I discovered an explanation for the pastor's sudden change: first, the carts were used exclusively for prostitution traffic; second, the only "blondes" in town were the prostitutes.

It was our one and only ride in those cute carts.

—Jack Aamot

# A Lady of Culture
# and Compassion

*Robert Maland*

Margo, a lady of culture and compassion, met Peter Wirth at the university in Zurich and moved to Brazil with her young husband. (See "The Man Called Peter," page 149.) When we met them in 1959, she was mother to their four children, the youngest being about three years old.

The Wirth family was among the first members of a new mission congregation that met in facilities attached to our home. For further outreach, we rented a storefront in a poor area of town where Margo and Peter extended their ministry.

This store, with its five-foot wide by ten-foot high doors of corrugated steel, when rolled up, provided us with another good place for evangelism. Many did come; some just dropped in when walking by. Street urchins stepped inside, apparently just to act up. But even some of these seemed to have had their hearts softened by the love of Jesus.

Most people in that area depended on employment in the coffee plantations. Unemployment could get extremely high during off season or when a rare but devastating frost came from the Antarctic. It was a most gratifying experience to be able to give them packages of crushed wheat and cans of vegetable oil from the USA Food for Peace Program.

Besides our food distribution, Margo came to this area to teach them how to plant vegetable gardens for healthier diets. Margo also left her comfortable millionaire's home with its swimming pool to teach the mothers and older daughters how to sew for their own needs and for extra income. Those same hands played the violin so beautifully at worship services. She often went to the orphanage in Oriente to teach the children domestic skills.

Margo, an accomplished musician, became the organist for the main congregation. She and Dr. Pedro invited girls from the orphanage to attend those services with their family. Each Sunday they also drove past the storefront in the poor neighborhood to offer a ride in their homemade recreation vehicle to anyone who wished to worship with them. When we last visited her in 1993, Dona Margo, now a widow, was continuing to do this. She was also teaching confirmation students during the Sunday school hour.

As a responsible Christian, long before it was politically correct, Margo demonstrated a concern for the care of God's earth. Both she and Dr. Pedro worked for preventing soil erosion and promoted reforestation. Under an extended roof on the back of their house, Margo planted a great variety of tree seedlings, caring for them in individual containers until they were large enough to be transplanted into larger containers. Finally, they would be planted in the place where she hoped they would continue to thrive.

In their agricultural ventures, Dona Margo and Dr. Pedro were concerned that seed be planted in good ground. What a privilege it was to be in kingdom partnership with them and observe that same concern that the seed, the Word of God, fall on good ground in the lives of Brazilians and others throughout the world.

# Part Four

## Faith Active
## In Love

# The High Cost of Poverty

*Andrew Olsen*

Chico was a house builder. He could not write his name, but he knew how to build the standard eighteen foot by eighteen foot batten board laborer's house from scratch. He needed no sketch or blueprint; it was all visualized in his head.

Someone gave a small parcel of land to the church for the building of a chapel in his laboring class vila. Friends in the United States sent one hundred and twenty dollars that paid for the material and the fence around the lot. Chico used his skills with joy and pride to build this chapel. There were no partitions inside.

We often had up to eighty persons at a service; seldom fewer than fifty. At the service of dedication, I brought people from another part of town in two trips of my Volkswagen bus. Heavy rains bombarded us that afternoon so I took all twenty-three back in one trip!

One Sunday when Chico arrived for worship services, he paid off a debt to another member, mentioning that he wanted to be free of all obligations. The following Tuesday he unexpectedly died of Chagas disease* at the age of forty-six. He had migrated to the new lands of Paraná from Minas Gerais State where the disease was endemic.

His widow decided that their nine-year-old son, Edimilson, had to quit third grade and spend time begging on the street to help support the family of six children. He was mentally sharp and academically strong. The second to the youngest child, he was the only one to go to school. We had been providing Edimilson's school uniform, shoes, and books.

But now, his mother insisted, if we were to keep him in school, we would also have to provide her with the amount he would have earned from begging. With regrets, we refused. There had to be a better solution. Unfortunately, his oldest sister moved to the state capital to become a prostitute and regularly sent money home to support the family. I fault the society not her. May God forgive this high cost of poverty.

\*

---

\* Chagas is a tropical disease caused by trypanosome, a parasite. The malady is marked by prolonged high fever, edema, and enlargement of the spleen, liver, and lymph nodes as well as undetected heart disease that usually results in a fatal heart attack at an early age.

# The One Needle

*Charles D. Eidum*

It was Dr. Lindolfo's* appointed Sunday to make the two hour drive with me to the Jacui parish for its monthly worship service. Although it was not intended to be a medical mission, it was to be a divine appointment.

Church council members of the large Ponta Grossa parish accompanied me to my eight outlying congregations to become better acquainted with our ministry.

A four-wheel drive vehicle was the best mode of transportation through the mountains and valleys to reach Jacui.

We usually made one stop to pick up the Butzke family who lived a long distance from the church. That day, however, no one was waiting. Being ahead of schedule, we descended the long hill to visit the Butzkes in their ramshackle home. Bruno and Martina and their five children welcomed us warmly.

To our horror, Rudi, the five-year-old son, had a massive blister that covered the top of his head. The doctor confided to me that if this boy didn't receive medical attention shortly, he would die.

We shared this medical evaluation and prognosis in private with the parents and Marisa, the oldest sister. Yet we were unable to convince Rudi to leave the security of his family to return with us to the big city hospital.

What were we to do? Finally Dr. Lindolfo said, "Now that we are here, let's at least try to save his life."

The parents hesitantly accepted Dr. Lindolfo's offer to perform the procedure he had outlined. He needed only two basics—hot water and a needle. Because they were drinking tea, the hot water was ready. The way the mother told Marisa, "Get the needle," I perceived they had only one.

We needed one more piece of equipment for this attempt to save a life—a table with straps to hold the patient. The doctor appointed me to serve as the vise on the kitchen table to hold Rudi's arms and legs while he punctured the blister.

The human vise was set. The frightened boy struggled like a cornered animal. As the needle pierced the blister, the pus shot out through the door and across the dirt yard. After removing as much of the putrid fluid matter as possible, the doctor instructed Marisa to shampoo her brother's head thoroughly every day and to cover his head with clean bandages. Marisa promised she would.

"It'll take a miracle for Rudi to live," Dr. Lindolfo sadly stated as we drove on to the church. "Even if the sister faithfully does her part, only God's intervention will make survival possible." We asked people to pray for Rudi.

The next month we left for Jacui a little earlier than usual. We approached the pickup spot in silence with a mixture of anticipation and apprehension. Much to our delight, among the passengers waiting at the side of the road was a smiling Rudi, proudly sporting a clean white bandage on his head.

We praised God who answers prayer and who grants a variety of ministries to function within his church.

---

\* The names have been changed.

# What Should We Do with All These Beans?

*Ron Baesler*

Six scruffy boys from the vila gathered around the full burlap sack. "What should we do with all these beans?" Ten months ago, who would have dreamed that they'd be asking that question? Ten months ago, who would have predicted the answer they gave?

It all started when Albertina and Elza, two widows who live in our shantytown, complained that the neighborhood kids "just run around and get into trouble." We discussed the complaint and finally decided that these kids had nothing to do but get into trouble.

One mother suggested, "Why not try a community garden?" Someone offered us a vacant lot; a farmer offered us bamboo for a fence; and the congregation gave a special offering to buy seed.

Now the trick was to link all these resources with the energy of the neighborhood kids. That was no easy task. Working together on a community project was a new experience for many people. Having grown up in a nearly feudal society where one works for the boss who takes care of you, which discourages initiative, these kids—like their parents—had a hard time seeing the value of such a project. But the soil was prepared. The very same two widows whose complaint had started it all kept hoeing and inviting.

Finally on September 7, Brazil's Independence Day, six of us cut bamboo, then dragged it a quarter of a mile to our garden. Before long a few more kids showed up, then more. Soon a bamboo brigade of fifteen was huffing and puffing across the fields. At noon, the four adults decided to quit for the day. But three boys asked me if they could come back and work in the afternoon too. Maybe a new seed was sprouting! Within a few days the fence was done and the seeds planted. During the days of waiting, the interest waned again. Once more Albertina and Elza kept things going, hoeing and fussing with the seedlings. But the kids seemed to have lost interest. They never showed up unless I did. I began to wonder if it was worth all the effort.

Then in early December the green beans started producing. "Come on, gang! Let's pick beans." A ragtag gang of six piled into our white Volkswagen bus for the two block ride to the garden. Within a half hour the sack was nearly full of beautiful long pods.

"What should we do with all these beans?" they asked. Alesandro remembered our first rule: Whoever works in the garden has the right to pick and eat. So we stopped at each little shack and filled a basin or a pot.

But the sack was still nearly half full. "What should we do with the rest?" I asked. Then little Daví, who had a runny nose and a ragged shirt—who had also thrown a stone at Albertina the previous week—looked at the beans and at his buddies and exclaimed, "I know! Let's give them to the poor!"

And so we did. My six little friends whom I considered poor, directed me to homes where people needed vegetables. With great joy and energy they gave away their beans.

Somehow they had learned something very important. They had learned to see the needs around them and to respond generously. They had done a very Christianlike thing. Yet many of them have very little contact with the church. We hold services regularly in the vila, but Daví and his friends haven't been very active. Yet somehow a seed had been planted in their lives. Somehow in dragging bamboo, hauling manure, and working alongside Elza and Albertina, the Spirit of the living Christ has begun to work.

# Whatever Happened to Carlos?

*M. Lorraine Foehringer*

L et's see if we can get Carlos off the farm," was the challenging decision of four men hosted in our home. Three American movie makers and Pastor Tony Halverson from Minneapolis were in Marília, São Paulo, in March 1970, at the request of the Division for World Mission of the American Lutheran Church. Their assignment was to make a *cinema verité* film to tell the story of the Lutheran mission in Brazil with candid realism.

My husband, Gene, had taken them to the farm where he conducted worship services twice a month. There they met shy nineteen-year-old Carlos and his parents, Senhor Valdomiro and Dona Emília. These sharecroppers lived with their three children in a primitive batten board shack with a dirt floor and a thatched roof.

Carlos had finished four years of school. Because he lived far from the city, however, he could not continue his education as he desired.

After their visit to the farm, these men discussed Carlos and his dead-end future. Their stated objective was, "Let's see if we can get Carlos off the farm."

One morning they picked up their equipment and left for the country to begin filming a story with no plot, not knowing how it would end. All this was very strange to Carlos, his family, and neighbors. His friends joked with him that now he was going to become a movie star.

As they were filming, Gene talked with Carlos about continuing his studies, much to the chagrin of his father who thought it was time for his son to marry and settle down.

With the filming complete, the men left for the United States to begin editing. The finished product was distributed under the title, *Carlos of Brazil*. This true-life, spontaneous story of a young man trapped in poverty, with no prospect of developing his abilities, stirred many throughout our church. Over the decades, many who remember the story have asked, "Whatever happened to Carlos?"

In February 1971, almost a year after the filming, Carlos came to live with us and begin his studies. It was a joy for me to have him in our home, helping him get ready for his further education. We outfitted him the best we could from the bales of clothing from Lutheran World Relief. Gifts of money helped purchase blankets, towels, pillow, and material for bedding. I sewed sheets, pillow cases, and a bedspread for Carlos. I taught him simple skills, such as how to make his bed.

A gift of money from an American enabled him to enroll in the Lutheran Bible School, Londrina, Paraná, in August of that same year. Parallel to that course, directed by Pastor James and Miriam Hougen, Carlos entered high school. When I came to Londrina for a women's meeting, he was so proud to show me his room—neat as a pin! It was a joy to see such progress.

Carlos finished his Bible course in 1974, but he continued to live at the Institute. He supported himself by working at a pharmacy during the day so he could complete his last year of high school at night. On Saturdays he did pastoral work at the prison. On Sundays, in the absence of the pastor, Carlos conducted the services at the Lutheran church.

In March 1976, he moved to the Internato Rural (Rural Dormitory) at Teófilo Otoni, Minas Gerais, where he was the housefather, supervisor, and educator for the poorest young people of that remote rural area. During this time Carlos received a degree in accounting. Next he participated in the course offered by the Lutheran Diaconal Association in Espírito Santo. In March 1978, Carlos was ordained a deacon of the Evangelical Church of the Lutheran Confession in Brazil.

Carlos married Célia Schuebel on January 6, 1979. They have been blessed with three children: Samuel, Miriam, and Jesse, now young adults and teenagers. Carlos and Célia have served together in a variety of missions, including ministering to an indigenous tribe. Presently they are administering the Creche Bom Samaritano, a day nursery for 160 infants in Pinhais, Paraná. The nursery is part of the Curitiba parish's social ministry among poor families.

Whatever happened to Carlos? Yes, he got off the farm, but more importantly, Carlos became a humble, winsome, effective servant, deeply committed to serving the least important ones in the name of his Lord Jesus.

### STRAIGHT FROM THE FARMER'S MOUTH

My husband, Bob, was a South Dakota farmer turned preacher. In one of his first sermons, on Jesus' figure of the vine and the branches, the key point was that the vine produces the fruit.

By misusing the word *galo* instead *galho* for branch, and *ovo* instead of *uva* for grapes, he enthusiastically preached that "it's the rooster that produces the egg."

—Ruth Kasperson

# What Do You Mean, We're Not Doing Social Work?

*Odin Kenneth Stenberg*

I had been in the city of Juiz de Fora about a month when Senhor Carlos asked to meet him at his office downtown. I was grasping for a handle on all that had to be done in that enormous evangelical community of south-central Brazil, and welcomed the chance to talk to the president of the parish council.

Carlos got right down to business. "Senhor Pastor, did you know we do social work here in Juiz de Fora? We get surplus wheat flour and other commodities from your country. The women of the Ladies Society divide up the sacks and cases of staple goods. You will take these food packets to our poor families in Vila Borboleta and São Pedro."

When I met Carlos for morning coffee some weeks later, Carlos was all smiles and enthusiasm about the "social-work" program. And I was glad they were making good use of these surplus food shipments to offer at least a minimum of life support to their most impoverished members.

But I had a problem with it and knew I would have to step around it gently.

I touched on the question by saying, "Senhor Carlos, I know it's a matter of sheer survival for the folks who are getting the help. But as I see it, we are not actually doing social work."

I might as well have thrown a firecracker into a haystack. Never a man to deal in subtlety, Carlos fairly exploded. "What do you mean, we're *not* doing social work?" I must have deflated an image of immense personal pride. Carlos flung the waitress forty centavos for the coffee and stormed out of the cafe.

Still smoldering, Carlos raised the social-work question at the next monthly meeting of the council and asked me to explain my bizarre definition of the social work they were doing.

"My brothers," I responded, "we all agree this distribution of food is absolutely essential. No doubt about that, but what is it costing us? Isn't it true that it's demanding nothing? Nothing of our time and energy? Nothing of personal sacrifices? Until we can bring these poor families to a place where they no longer need these humiliating handouts, I don't think we can call it social work."

The men listened politely but their faces mirrored a barely tolerant impatience and general disagreement. I could all but hear them saying, "So now what do we have here? Another crazy notion in the head of this Yankee norte-americano?"

I went on looking for a way to move things along, to put wheels under what I had been trying to tell them. One day I received a gift of fifty dollars from a seminary buddy in the United States, with instructions: "Use it any way you want."

I asked Carlos if he knew of a family in dire need of help. Without a moment of hesitation he told me about Oskar Kappel, one of the men on the fourteen-member parish council who was having an extremely difficult time financially.

Senhor Oskar had lost his job when a local stocking industry failed and shut down. He was the man who had maintained the machines, knew every step in the production process. When the company closed he had to take a menial position as a quality-control inspector in a shoe factory. The job left him so destitute he could not even sandal his barefoot wife and children.

I began meeting with the Kappel family on Monday nights to get to know them and to focus on a series of graphic flip charts called *Conversas Sôbre a Fé Cristã* ("Conversations about the Christian Faith"). In these nonthreatening discussions with the family, I discovered that Oskar was a grandson of an immigrant German engineer who responded to a once-upon-a-time call by the Emperor Dom Pedro II to open up the vast interior of the country with roads and bridges.

His wife, Dona Carolina, was a pretty, olive-skinned *Baiana* (from the state of Bahia). She was trim, bright, and attractive—but illiterate. In her native north-east Brazil, school is for the family of the *fazendeiro*, the "landlord". The children of the farm laborers have to work in the cotton fields.

The six Kappel children ranged up the ladder from an infant to a girl of thirteen. Oskar, Carolina and the children all sat in a circle on the solidly packed dirt floor, read the Portuguese New Testament week after week, and lingered over the promises of Jesus, who was offering a life that could lighten the darkness.

I asked Oskar if he had any skills. "I have one," he said. "I know how to make stockings." His eyes lit up as he confided a long, long dream to have his own knitting machine. I wondered if there was any way it could happen.

We talked about it, and Oskar explained, "The owner of the abandoned factory where I used to work as a technician would gladly sell off his machines, at half price or less. But," he lamented, "I don't have any money."

I inquired how much one of them would cost. Oskar cited an approximate figure in cruzeiros. I calculated the rate of exchange, to see what the fifty-dollar gift from the United States might bring at the money exchange. Those fifty dollars would multiply into fifty thousand cruzeiros! Enough to buy one machine.

At the next meeting of the council I proposed the beginning of a parish-wide credit union, to be managed by the officers of the council. I offered to turn over the mission gift as the initial capital, suggested asking a return at a low rate of interest, and recommended Senhor Oskar as the first to receive assistance. The men considered the offer, asked a few procedural questions, and gave their unanimous consent. Oskar sat at the far end of the table with his head in his hands, fighting back the tears.

Oskar ran into various roadblocks: The Kappel house had a dirt floor and no room for the half-ton knitting machine, which had to be anchored in concrete. Then an obliging neighbor offered the use of a backroom lean-to, where Oskar could pour a slab of cement, bolt down the machine, and start the minimal new industry. A downtown supplier with whom Oskar had formerly dealt provided a case of cotton spindles on credit.

Then there was a seeming eternity of late-night toil and struggle to recondition the old machine to make it produce. Finally, one early morning, a proud and smiling Carolina had a bundle of new stockings to sell at the neighborhood's open-air street market. Every penny went back into other spindles of mercerized cotton, general maintenance, and a monthly payment to the credit union.

A little over a year after the venture began, Oskar brought his last installment to the council and had set aside enough to buy a second machine. Oskar and the men of the council stood and joined in a song of rousing celebration!

Dona Petronilha, a wealthy spinster in the parish, heard what the Kappels had done and volunteered to double the balance in the credit-union treasury. This meant there would also be help for other needy families. A fledgling enterprise was feathering out and starting to fly.

Oskar taught his wife and their daughter, Olgina, how to tend the machines during the day while he was at the shoe factory. At night he ran the operation alone—on into the wee hours. It was still a rocky road for the Kappels, but hope was overtaking despair.

One family in the parish contracted with the council to add a room to the Kappel's house.

My family and I returned to the United States when our mission term ended. Missionary colleagues, Pastor John and Valerie Westby, came from the interior of São Paulo to take over the work in Juiz de Fora.

Years later I questioned John about the Kappels. He shared the good news, "Senhor Oskar is doing well now. Each of his sons and daughters has received a good education. All of them have jobs and professions. Oskar can never talk about the years you had together without crying."

Looking back on those difficult and challenging years, my wife, Carola, and I asked ourselves, "So what have we learned from all this?" Clearly, at least one thing: Small can be beautiful.

---

* Edited from the unpublished novel, *Islands on a Wide Sea,* by Odin Kenneth Stenberg. (Copyright 1997) Used by permission.

# A Field Day for Skeptics

*Donald Nelson*

Some called us crazy idealists. At times I suspected they were right. But the skeptics did have a three year field day with our project of establishing a Lutheran school in Campo Novo de Parecis in the newly colonized area of Mato Grosso State, in central-west Brazil.

The school project was not really the dream of any one person; nor was it born out a burning passion to find a way to serve the community. Rather it was a seed planted in May 1994, with a casual observation by Bishop Gerd Kliewer when he installed me as the first pastor of this developing parish. In his message the bishop stated that he saw no private, nongovernment school in our city. That was all. It was neither a call to mission, nor the setting of a goal.

But we did not forget his comment. It proved to be like a single mustard seed that Jesus spoke about (Mark 4:30–32), one that forces itself up through hard ground, fighting to establish roots and strong branches to eventually provide a needed nesting place.

The solitary seed sprouted two months later when eighteen of our one hundred eighty baptized members braved a stormy night to gather to discuss this issue. Mrs. Irena Horst moved that we appoint a committee to study the possibility of planting a school. Although it was unanimously approved, many, including myself, had little idea what lay ahead. Most of us envisioned a one- or two-room schoolhouse alongside the church, typical of many rural congregations.

Five months later, Professor Dorival Fleck, director of the department of education of the Evangelical Church of the Lutheran Confession in Brazil (IECLB), visited our congregation. He came to discourage the committee from pursuing pipe dreams. But after four days with us, he gave his studied opinion that a school should be implemented in our city of seven thousand people. In the presence of twenty-five municipal and church leaders, he clarified that the project must receive broad public support and that all citizens, not just Lutherans, would have to want the school.

He left, but his insights remained. Although we only partially understood the implications, they proved to be wise. He stated, first, that there was no longer a market in the Brazilian educational field for a one-room school that gradually expands to a full elementary school. From the beginning we would need to offer the equivalent of grades K-12. Second, the school must offer quality, not only in the classroom instruction, but in the facility and staff. To the scoffers, this was a greater pipe dream.

Next the committee invited architect-engineer Dr. Margaret Introvini to proceed with initial design of a building for 550 students. At that time we had neither money nor promise of financial help from any source and no official backing of the church except our local, struggling congregation. Another field day for skeptics.

We began to sense an urgency for action, however. The department of education had received fourteen different inquiries about the feasibility of starting a private school in our city. If we did not move quickly, we would face competition. Dr. Introvini, in consultation with Professor Fleck, presented a plan for the construction of a complete facility, including an auditorium and a special building for preschool children.

Fortunately, at this crucial time, encouragement came unexpectedly in a casual conversation while sipping *chimarrão* (matte tea) with a local farmer. He offered us nearly a city block in his soybean field at the end of the city's main avenue! His business sense was correct. Land values go up when a school is located nearby. We did not question his motives; we accepted the offer.

In July 1995, a contractor, Clecir Keller, arrived in the city to build a fine home for a lumber baron. Seeing his good work, we contracted him even though we still had no money in our bank account or under mattresses.

Help came through a friend of the mission, Mr. Roger Eggen, a Lutheran businessman in Minneapolis, who agreed to loan a portion of the money needed to get water and electricity installed and the foundation laid. When bean prices dramatically fell, several civic leaders met to discuss the financial future of the school project in light of the worst economic year in our young county's seven year history.

We agreed that any legal way of raising funds would be acceptable. By this time we had succeeded in convincing some people that this would indeed be a school for the public, although administered by Lutherans. This was a crucial point for enlisting civic and church support.

In August 1995, with the assistance of a local farmer who had contacts in the capital, committee members were able to speak briefly with the governor and received his approval for a $30,000 grant. The money was delayed, but we finally received it.

Another milestone gave the doubters more reason to ridicule. We contracted Professor Paul Edison Knüppe to be director. Together with his wife and son, he left southern Brazil to take on the impossible task of opening our school in March 1997, with no funds and a building whose walls were raised three feet. He was a director with no school. Our parish graciously loaned him the parsonage; my wife and I went to live on the outskirts of town. Professor Paul worked on obtaining official authorizations, hiring teachers, and recruiting students.

Because the original committee had completed its mission, it disbanded and turned the continuation over to the new school board.

As the board faced difficult times, they remembered that ignorance promotes death and learning is tied up with life. Encouragement came through the theme of the Lutheran Church for that year, the words of Jesus, "I came that they may have life, and have it abundantly" (John 10:10 NRSV). We became more convinced that a confessional school was not a luxury but a necessity in our city in order to influence decisions made here, and not least in the area of ecology.

The Lutheran Educational Institute of Parecis began classes on March 3, 1997 in the parish hall of the Roman Catholic Church. We began with ten teachers and seven first year high school students. Of the seven, only one was Lutheran. This ratio may well continue into the future. On May 12 the school moved into its new permanent building of seven classrooms.

I know that I could never do this again. But I am grateful for the opportunity to have walked with people in political, as well as educational, arenas.

Through the work of faith and labor of love of many determined people, the persistent mustard seed grew to be a sapling, struggling to become a strong tree, so that many may nest in its large branches.

# Now They've Killed the Rich Man's Cow

*Ron Baesler*

Ademir was a blond, thin, twenty-year-old Brazilian of German descent. He had been the president of the youth group in the country congregation where he used to live. His father was a land-less farm worker. The tiny house they lived in was their own. The tiny plot of land around it belonged to them too. But the land the family cultivated and sweated over was not their own. They were sharecroppers. Sharecropping is always a low-return effort, but when the price of soybeans kept dropping while prices of fertilizers and pesticides and food kept rocketing upward, Ademir's family began to wonder if it was all worth it.

Finally they decided to join the *Movimento dos Sem Terra,* the Landless Farm Workers Movement. This group has been struggling for decades to promote a redistribution of land in Brazil where vast tracts of land lie unused, held by state and federal governments or owned by wealthy city dwellers as a hedge against inflation.

This movement keeps before all of us the will of God as expressed in Psalm 24: "The earth is the Lord's and all that is in it." If the earth is the Lord's, then the earth does not exist primarily to guarantee wealth for the already wealthy. If the earth is the Lord's, then the earth exists to sustain and give life.

But as Ademir and his family discovered, the will of God meets with tremendous resistance in a world accustomed to making its own rules and guaranteeing its own privileges.

Despite the fact that land reform is explicitly written into the Brazilian constitution; despite the fact that millions of acres of arable land lie untouched; despite the fact that all major cities are already surrounded by slums full of people who have left the rural areas; despite all of this, the landless poor who want to work and produce food for their families and their country are resisted every step of the way.

Ademir and his family spent two and a half years living in a tent made of black plastic. They camped alongside a federal highway together with thousands of other families. They participated in public protests, meetings, conferences, pilgrimages, and in marches to the state capital. They did what they could to force the government to keep its promises.

Of course they were portrayed in the media as "anarchists, communists, and lazy bums who want something for nothing." Very few people here believe that any group of people can organize and change Brazilian society. Those who try are a threat and therefore must be discredited lest the rest of society be put to shame. Add that pressure to the tremendous power of the rich landowners, and you begin to see how difficult any land reform can be.

But inspired very directly by biblical stories like the Exodus, the Movement does not give up. Sheer persistence paid off. On December 9, 1991, Ademir and his family, along with thirty other families, finally were resettled on eight hundred acres of state owned land next to our town of Guaíba, Rio Grande do Sul.

As a last act of vindictive violence, the state police confiscated the tools of the settlers when they left their campsite along the highway. They arrived in Guaíba with their black plastic tents, their families, and little else.

The government promised them food until they could harvest their first crops. But the promises were not kept. They worked hard, planting when they could get seed, even though it was very late in the planting season. They dug a well by hand. They received with gratitude what local churches could provide.

Meanwhile a rich rancher continued running his one hundred and twenty head of cattle on what was now their land. Finally, one day in desperation, they penned up twelve cattle. When the rancher showed up, they told him, "Look, we don't want to hurt your cattle. We are doing this to call the government's attention to our plight. It's a form of protest."

The rancher seemed agreeable. He said, "I can see you are suffering. I sympathize with you and will even donate a cow for you to butcher."

But the farmers protested, "Butchering a cow will solve our problem for a few days. But we want the government to keep its promise to us. If you want to help, join us in our protest."

Now it was the rancher's turn to protest. "No, I can't do that. You see, I've run my cattle on this land for years without paying rent to the state. I can't call attention to myself without getting into trouble."

It was an impasse between desperate, hungry people and a rich rancher. The rancher left and in frustration the farmers decided to accept his offer. They killed one of the cows and started dressing it.

In the middle of the operation the rancher returned with the police. Twenty men were arrested; the women and children were terrorized. Eleven men spent the night in jail and were released pending a hearing. Was this a setup? A trap? A misunderstanding? Why wasn't the fact that the slaughtered beef was divided up and kept by the police reported in the news?

Ademir and his family did not know the answers to these questions. But they insist that this arrest and the constant harassment are natural consequences of the struggle for justice and dignity.

Most members of our congregation were uneasy, however. They were willing to donate used clothes and food to these people. "But now they have killed the rich man's cow," they reasoned. "They disobeyed the law of the land and challenged the authorities."

The question persists, "Will we be able to stand in solidarity alongside these people who do not submit to the corruption and indifference of the government?"

A few days before Passion Sunday our women's group went out to the farmers' settlement. We listened and asked questions. We shared our faith. We again thought about what it means to carry the cross in a belligerent, selfish world. Together we reflected upon the cross of Christ whose death marked the ultimate act of solidarity with suffering people.

We continue to pray that others will join us in celebrating the resurrection of this crucified Christ, who plants the living seed of hope in all, who—like Ademir—carry crosses in Brazil and the world.

## MOLDED TOGETHER

Otto Tollefson, serving in Joinville, nationally noted for its malleable iron foundry, *Fundição Tupy,* made certain he wrote down the name of a visiting drama and music group from the Evangelical Foundation, *Fundação Evangélica.* But the college students laughingly insist he still introduced them to his congregation as the Evangelical Foundry—the name they adopted for the rest of their tour.

# Fridolino's Mission

*Charles D. Eidum*

Fridolino* was busy tallying the Sunday morning offering when I reminded him that he was scheduled to go with me to the Jacui congregation that afternoon. At first he hesitated and searched for a pretext. Then, recognizing that it would only be an excuse, he decided to get this little obligation out of the way. "Sure, pastor, when will you pick me up?" was his forced reply.

Little did we know that Fridolino's visit would launch a specialized ministry that would continue for many years.

I had challenged members of the church council of my large urban parish to accompany me whenever I went to one of the eight scattered congregations and preaching points. It was an attempt to build better relationships and sense of oneness in ministry within the parish.

Instead of it being a one-time encounter with the people in the mountainous back country, Fridolino saw so many needs that when he returned that night to his comfortable home, he was unable to sleep.

The next day Fridolino made a surprise visit to the parsonage even though he knew it was my day off. He almost begged to go on the next trip. He said that he did not want to be the only extra person, however.

179

No longer did I have to recruit men to go into the interior; now it became Fridolino's mission. He began the process of developing a meaningful ministry to meet the needs of some of the poorest people in the area.

He became the self-appointed chauffeur of the four-wheel drive vehicle carrying the parish worker to conduct confirmation classes and lead the women's Bible study groups. He volunteered to drive me to conduct the worship and minister to parishioners and friends in the outlying areas.

Either packed into that car, or following behind in a Volkswagen Kombi, were materials and a team of men to do special projects, such as building a chimney in the house for a 100-year-old man. The Kombi often took a longer way home because it couldn't climb the mountains. But there were always people ready to carry out the project outlined for them to accomplish that particular Sunday.

The four-wheeler seldom returned to Ponta Grossa without transporting one or more hundred-pound sacks of dried brown beans. Fridolino sold the beans at a good price in town in order to bring back cash or the purchases requested by the struggling farm families.

Fridolino learned some lessons the hard way, such as the necessity of selling clothes for a nominal price instead of giving them away. When he visited a family who had received free clothing, he discovered that the lady of the house had thrown the clothes over a nearby knoll when they got too soiled. She didn't want to wash them, thinking she would be receiving more free ones.

Fridolino matured as he helped the other men and their families in the congregation to grow in their Christian stewardship, teaching them that giving is more than money; real stewardship is the giving of oneself. In the process many of the poorest were blessed and learned how to become a blessing to others.

---

\*    The name has been changed.

# The Philippian Connection

*Richard Wangen*

Although the people of Harvey, North Dakota, have never met the Surui indigenous people of Brazil, and the Surui have never met the good people of Harvey, there is a vital connection between them that I call the *Philippian connection*.

And it is understandable if North Americans find Harvey, Rondônia, and Acre to be places equally unknown to them. For me, Harvey was home, as it had been for my parents and grandparents. Grandpa and Grandma Wangen came from Norway, homesteaded in Harvey, and helped build the Lutheran Church. Today it is also home to some 600 baptized members of First Lutheran Church, mostly farmers, who have maintained a long-term, far-reaching relationship with mission work in Brazil.

First Lutheran Church is more than a home congregation to my wife, Dorothy, and me. It is our "Philippian congregation", for we have received love and dedication from them as the apostle Paul received from the Philippian believers. Like Paul, we have great affection for this community of caring Christians in their mission outreach. No other image fits as well to describe the wonderful, trusting relationship that we celebrated through the four decades of our mission work in Brazil.

It is that Philippian relationship that eventually impacted the lives of Roberto Zwetsch and Lori Altmann. Roberto now holds the chair of missiology at the Lutheran seminary in São Leopoldo, Rio Grande do Sul. Lori has been active in mission among the scattered native people who have left their villages. The long mission trek of Roberto and Lori is the fruit of this Philippian relationship with the mission-concerned members of the Harvey congregation.

Roberto was born in a Lutheran family of German ancestry in the nearby industrial port city of Porto Alegre. While yet a young-ster his parents moved to Caxias do Sul, where Pastor Robert Maland was developing a mission congregation. The elder Zwetsches described it as a time when their faith moved from nomi-nal Lutheranism to a dynamic, growing relationship with Christ. Roberto received his confirmation instruction from Pastor Maland. Later the family moved to Curitiba, Paraná.

It was there that I first met Roberto, while I was serving as youth and campus pastor. He became an active member of our youth group. I remember clearly a moment of deep reflection on his part while we were on a youth outing to an island. Our focus was on the message of 1 John 4:7–21. Roberto's life was impacted by verses 19–21 (NRSV):

> We love because he first loved us. Those who say, "I love God", and hate their brothers or sisters, are liars; for those who do not love a brother or sister whom they have seen, cannot love God whom they have not seen. The commandment we have from him is this: those who love God must love their brothers and sisters also.

From that moment Roberto moved on to a deeper faith in-volvement.

Roberto and I met again after I had been called in 1971 to the chair of pastoral care at the theological seminary of the Evangeli-cal Church of the Lutheran Confession in Brazil (IECLB). I was one of his professors during his years of preparing for the pastoral ministry. It was then that he mentioned his desire to be a missionary among the Brazilian native people. At that time there was no Brazilian Lutheran ministry (IECLB) to Native Brazilians.

However, for Roberto to have a voice in following his call to mission, he needed to be free of dependency on financial aid from the Brazilian church. He was able to choose to be a missionary among the Brazilian Indians because of the scholarship that I had the privilege of arranging from the Harvey congregation. This financial aid was over and above their normal contributions to the synod and church-wide bodies.

For six years, First Lutheran faithfully supported Roberto in his theological preparation to be a Brazilian missionary among Brazilian Indians, and an extended year of study in northern Brazil. It was truly a trust relationship, and Roberto was faithful to God's call. Our Philippian partnership paid off in greater fruit for mission.

I officiated at the marriage of Roberto and Lori. Besides her theological degree, Lori has a master's in religious science and is now studying anthropology.

Upon their graduation from the Lutheran seminary, they were sent as missionaries by the IECLB to the Surui in Rondônia, in the Amazon River basin. The reservation had been abandoned by the National Indian Foundation (FUNAI), and the health of the Surui was seriously jeopardized. Because the lives of these indigenous people were of no value to the military dictatorship, they considered Roberto and Lori's attempt to develop native leadership to be meddling. Government authorities expelled the couple from the reservation. Eventually another Lutheran missionary came to serve the Surui.

Nevertheless, the expulsion did not discourage Roberto and Lori. They remained true to their call. Soon they received a call from the IECLB to serve the Kulina people in the state of Acre, bordering Peru, where they served for seven years. During this time their second child was born on the reservation, delivered in the cultural manner of the mother squatting. A member of the village cut the umbilical cord and the newborn received his name, Binou, according to the custom of the Kulina people.

It was through these two experiences—living with the Surui and Kulina people—that the Zwetsches developed a definite theology of mission, which oriented his later studies in missiology and his teaching of missions at the seminary today. His theology of mission can be called a mission of conviviality, or the "Christian witness of a living and responsible presence".

The Kulina village, where Roberto and Lori spent seven years, already had a mission history when they arrived. Contact with Europeans had already been made some sixty years before when the rubber-tappers used the Brazilian Indians as slave labor. Later there was mission work done by itinerant Catholic priests; and some years back, from the Peruvian side, there was evangelization by the Wycliffe Bible Translators. There were even native preachers. So Roberto and Lori entered into a potpourri of religions. When they left, there continued to be a Christian congregation. Another Lutheran missionary followed them and is there at the present time.

We are proud of Roberto and Lori's capable, clear, and courageous contribution to our teaching staff. They combine an excellent balance of the two thrusts of the ministry of Jesus. Their concern demonstrates the compassion of Jesus for those who suffer the effects of social dysfunction; but on the other hand, they are conscious of the fact that suffering has a cause. So they courageously confront the demonic systems, as Jesus did with his symbolic acts of healing.

Roberto and Lori are loved and respected by the 300 students at the seminary in São Leopoldo. Their experience and living-Gospel apprenticeship is certainly a credit and joy to the trust relationship and financial support of the Philippian connection established by the Harvey community.

# Loops, Buffers, Pills, and Shots

*Andrew Olsen*

The mayor's first words were encouraging, "Do it, pastor!" But then, as a practicing obstetrician-gynecologist, he added, "Just don't tell me anything! Remember, I don't know anything."

It was a direct response to my consultation with him about the possibility of my conducting a birth control seminar for medical personnel. It was at a time when birth control devices were not readily available. Also it was illegal—at least on the books—to sell or provide them.

We were concerned about the high incidence of abortions being used as birth control, however, especially among the poorer class. One woman we knew claimed to have had thirteen abortions—none by a medical practitioner.

It led me first to investigated the use of Lippes Loop intrauterine device (IUD). I translated into Portuguese material from the U.S. Health Department regarding the use of IUDs in Puerto Rico. Then I gave an informal seminar for a small group of doctors on the front lawn of our home. Each received a copy of the study. Dr. Jonas Kimura, a general practitioner, agreed to install the devices free of charge for the needy women we brought to him.

My mother smuggled the IUDs to me through the mail, one or two at a time, rolled up inside *Time* magazines. The same method was used for obtaining benzalkonium chloride, the disinfectant agent used with the loop.

About fifteen poor women, all who had had previous abortions, received the loops. Since the women had never been to a doctor, it was necessary for my wife, Ardys, to accompany them during the medical procedure, so they could be assured nothing would go wrong.

A colleague asked me how these IUDs worked. When I explained that they prevent the fertilized egg from attaching itself to the uterine wall, he concluded that it was essentially an early abortion. I agreed it was, but that it was a much safer and less life-threatening procedure than would otherwise be used.

Our relationship with the medical community was one of mutual help and respect. When an anesthesiologist needed new "airways," my mother sent them in.

A local pediatrician kept me supplied with a gallon jar of worm pills that I readily gave out on my pastoral visits, especially among the poor farm and vila residents.

In my briefcase I carried DPT shots, each one costing twenty-seven cents, and syringes that I boiled before and after use. About one out of ten who received the first shot, received the whole series, usually because the parents claimed the child had run a fever after the first shot. The prevailing attitude was that all persons should get whooping cough when they are young so they are over it for the rest of their lives.

When a medical lab was set up in Paranavai, I helped the young owner with the donation of a floor buffer we no longer used. I only asked that they provide free feces exams whenever I or my family needed one, or when I sent a member to get one. They agreed. We got our money's worth. They once said that if they were to become believers, they would choose our God.

# Grandpa Gene Had a Dream

*M. Lorraine Foehringer*

The Project began with a grandpa playing checkers with street kids and grew to include the daily feeding of three hundred and fifty children and the employment of fifty persons who could offer hope to kids and parents alike. The grandpa was my husband, Pastor Eugene Foehringer, a few years away from retirement.

When we moved to Lapa, a suburb of São Paulo, in 1975, we were appalled with the number of children living on the streets. He was called to pastor the Central Lutheran parish, with its church sandwiched in between skyscrapers. The building faced a never-ending flow of traffic of buses, cars, and people, hurrying like ants intent on making a living. But throughout this bustling megalopolis of sixteen million people, there are an estimated 800,000 who are classified as "street kids."

Joseph A. Page aptly describes the situation:

> The universe of "street kids" in Brazil breaks down into two categories: those who actually live on the streets and sleep on the sidewalks, under viaducts, or in other sheltered locations, and those who sleep at home but roam the streets during the day. Some work, some play, some beg, some sniff glue, and some engage in criminal activity that ranges from petty theft to armed assault to an occasional murder.*

Gene was moved by Godlike compassion to become a friend to those street kids. He began by spending one day a week on the streets of the Lapa *bairro,* talking with the children and playing checkers with them. He got to know them and their problems. He took them to the doctor when necessary and sometimes to the police where he served as their advocate. The city council gave him a permit to help in this one-day-a-week outreach to the street kids.

Instead of coasting his last years to retirement, Gene was captivated by a Spirit-inspired dream, as God had said through the prophet Joel, "your old men shall dream dreams." In December 1985, he resigned as parish pastor so that he could devote himself to a full-time ministry among the abandoned minors.

We had learned that in the 1960s, land had been donated to the Lutheran parish in Santo Amaro, one of the largest suburbs that make up Greater São Paulo. This property was far from the church and the life of its members. Some women of that parish, however, together with their pastor, had begun an outreach with social and educational programs in a slum near the donated land. Given that slum-dwellers seldom if ever allow outsiders, including police, religious, and social workers, to venture into a slum, the location was a godsend. It was because of this initial work that Pastor Gene and the Santo Amaro Church got together to pursue a common dream.

The birth of this dream was not without pain and tears. Although all the pastors and churches of the Evangelical Church of the Lutheran Confession in Brazil (IECLB) in the São Paulo area showed much interest and gave needed support, Gene's own Central parish gave little encouragement or help in the beginning.

Pastor Kathryn Lee, area secretary for the division of global mission of the Evangelical Lutheran Church in America (ELCA), worked out an agreement between the ELCA and the IECLB whereby ELCA funds would be used to underwrite the pastoral ministry of The Project for the Reconciliation of the Minor.

The purpose of this new work was to make possible a life with dignity for these poor children and give them opportunities for a better life in the future. It was to be a united community project that would not exclude anyone.

Gene often explained, "We want to be a voice for the child who is forgotten and abandoned."

The Project began work with the local families. Gene was officially called by the church council to begin this new missionary work. On April 7, 1986, The Project was officially born. A flurry of activities followed, and financial campaigns were launched. We first built a stucco wall around the property, then cleared and prepared it for construction. We applied for the necessary legal papers and bureaucratic licenses so that construction could begin.

On October 10, the first activities were begun. We ordered blueprints drawn for a simple shelter so there would be a place to conduct the first classes. We offered instruction in knitting, crocheting, and ceramics. To help mothers increase their income without leaving their homes, we trained them to be beauticians. We supervised the children in doing their homework. This not only prepared them to become productive persons but kept them in school and off the streets during their formative years.

In December, a group was formed to work in a makeshift kitchen, initially serving forty meals a day to children whose mothers worked outside the home. At this point all the teachers and helpers were volunteers. Among these was Teresinha. She also baked cakes for birthdays and special occasions—the first time many children had such personal recognition. She is still with The Project and is now a paid worker, as are her husband, Anésio, and all the workers.

On December 7, 1987, we held an open-air worship service of joyful dedication, which was attended by people from the community, members of the Lutheran churches, and representatives of the Catholic church.

By April 1988 we completed the construction of a house where a caretaker could live and the first classes could be offered. Worship services could now be held on a regular basis. In July, we received $75,000 from Central Lutheran, Winona, Minnesota, that enabled us to buy a house under construction, adjacent to the original property, increasing available space for classrooms and activities.

During this time a proposal was written and submitted to the IECLB for approval, to seek funding from entities in the United States and Germany.

A year later, on April 11, 1989, Gene suffered a ruptured aorta and was rushed to the Heart Institute where emergency surgery gave him a one chance in ten to live. By God's grace and the skill of the medical personnel, Gene survived the surgery. Unfortunately, it was necessary for him to resign from the work of The Project. He had worked so hard to have The Project established on a firm foundation before his planned retirement in September of that year.

Fortunately, Pastor Dirk Oesselmann, a theological intern from Germany at the Santo Amaro Church, who had been helping Gene about twice a week, assumed the full-time directorship. When Pastor Dirk moved to northern Brazil to begin a similar work with the children, Pastor Wilhelm Nordmann, also from Germany, was called to continue the work.

We soon recognized that a greater need existed than providing for the immediate needs of the street kids; it was to help and encourage the families of the area. Difficult, dysfunctional family situations are a major cause of children being abandoned or left to roam the streets. To address this, The Project has made available to adolescents and adults classes in woodworking, carpentry, keyboarding, the use of computers, sewing, crafts, and recycling paper. This helps guarantee future employment and often brings the participants immediate cash benefits. There are literacy classes for adults and general discussion groups to help them develop awareness of their problems and deal with them effectively.

Programs and activities for children and adolescents include tutoring in school work and participation in theater, puppets, *capoeira,* (an agile, foot-fighting dance), sports, and crafts.

Today The Project serves three meals a day to 350 children. Children are now getting a clean bill of health at their periodic health exams. Every day during school vacation, Anésio takes a Volkswagen Kombi load of children, ranging in ages from three to seventeen, down the mountains to the beautiful beaches in Santos for swimming and fun.

There is a staff of fifty paid employees, some part-time. Volunteers teach crocheting and knitting to adults. A full-time instructor teaches woodworking and painting of the objects produced. In December 1993, representatives from the ELCA pledged financial support for the pastoral leadership for a five year period. Contributions continue to come from friends in the United States and Germany.

Informal worship services are conducted for the children, parents, and residents of that area. Music is provided by guitar and violin. Bible studies are offered to adults. During the week children have religion classes that include Bible stories and singing.

Gene was touched deeply by one little girl who liked to sit on his lap and stroke his beard. Because of skin cancer he grew a beard to help protect him from the hot sun. The girl said, "I can't call you daddy as I have a daddy, but I don't know where he is." Later when she was returning from school, she was struck and killed by an automobile. Gene was heartbroken.

I sewed a layette for a couple with one infant who came from Northeast Brazil with absolutely nothing. They lived in a one-room shack with a dirt floor, a bed, and a stove. I made twelve diapers, a flannel blanket, and some other pieces. The wife was overwhelmed with joy as she had only one diaper. Imagine, a whole dozen!

At the 1994 annual meeting, an official council was formed. Although at this time the name was changed to the Community Program for the Reconciliation of the Minor, it is still popularly called The Project. A committee and the pastors from Santo Amaro Church have continued giving their untiring help and influence as they did from the beginning.

Pastor Gene passed from this life on February 26, 1990. Gene did not get to retire in Brazil, which was his deep desire, but he died doing what he loved. Fifteen minutes before he died in the Stanford University Medical Center, Palo Alto, California, a packet of letters and cards, written and made by the children from The Project, came to his beside. He did not see them because he was in a coma.

When I returned to Brazil following Gene's death, I visited The Project. All those black eyes looked at me in wonderment. Gene had been there one day, and the next day he was gone forever. They never saw him again. I was being comforted by comforting them. At their request, I presented them with an enlarged picture of Gene to hang in their office as the founder of The Project. He loved those children as his own grandchildren, and they loved him.

In January 1993, the Children's Corner was inaugurated in another slum area as a branch of The Project.

In July 1997, the Theater Group of eight adolescents, three adults directors, and Pastor Takeshi of the Japanese Lutheran Church of São Paulo, traveled to Japan at the invitation of a group of Japanese who had visited The Project. The youth gave sixteen presentations of their drama that deals with the problem of street children.

The Project continues to minister to hundreds of children. For example, Sheila, fourteen, is alone in the world and full of problems. Her mother died when she was born; she does not know who her father is. She was given to an aunt and grandmother to raise; both have since died. Sheila left Northeast Brazil and made her way to São Paulo, searching for a place where she would be valued as a human being. Neighbors directed her to The Project where she receives free psychological counseling, training courses, and food. She tells her friends, "There is a place for me at The Project."

Gene's ministry was such that The Project was well-grounded and has continued to grow so that children are not forgotten and abandoned to roam the streets.

A grandpa's Spirit-inspired dream had not only been born but has captured the vision and ongoing support of God's people.

---

* *The Brazilians* (Reading, MA: Addison-Wesley Publishing Company, Inc., 1995), 260.

# Contributors

(All sponsoring congregations listed are Lutheran)

Abbreviations for states in Brazil:

RS=Rio Grande do Sul;
SC=Santa Catarina;
PR=Paraná;
SP=São Paulo;
GB=Guanabara;
MT=Mato Grosso

**Pastor Jack and Ruth Aamot** served in Paranavaí, PR; Novo Hamburgo, RS. Sponsoring congregations: Our Saviour's, Jackson; Calvary, Golden Valley, MN.

**Pastor John H. and Ruby L. Abel** served in Cianorte, Londrina, Campo Mourão, and Curitiba, PR. They were supported by the World Mission Prayer League, the Evangelical Lutheran Church, American Lutheran Church, and Association of Lutheran Free Congregations.

**Pastor Louis and Agnes Becker** served in Dracena and São Paulo, SP; Cianorte, PR; Joinville, SC. Sponsoring congregations: Oak Grove, Minneapolis; Westwood, St. Louis Park; Trinity, Hayfield, MN and First, Minot, ND.

**Pastor Ron and Lin Baesler** served in Morro Redondo, Estéio-Sapucaia, and Guaíba, RS. Sponsoring congregations: First,

Williston; Peace, Fargo; Augustana, Grand Forks; Grafton, Grafton; St. John's, Hatton; Elim, Fargo, ND; Grace, Ada; Our Savior's, Canby, MN; Immanuel, Swea City, IA.

**Pastor Clifford and Donna Biel** served in Loanda and Maringá, PR.

**Pastor Charles and Edna Eidum** served in Ponta Grossa, PR.

**Pastor Robert and Lola Fedde** served in Cianorte, Umuarama, Cascavel, and Ponta Grossa, PR; Rio de Janeiro, GB. Among their sponsoring congregations were Oak Knoll, Golden Valley; Bethlehem, Mankato, MN; St. Matthew's, Beaverton, OR.

**Pastor Eugene and M. Lorraine Foehringer** served in Marília and São Paulo, SP. Sponsoring congregations: Congregations of Root River Conference, S.E. MN; Central, Winona; Rushford, Rushford; Plummer, Plummer, MN; Oceanside, Long Island, NY.

**Pastor Glenn and Janel Hetland** served in Paranavaí, PR and Passo Fundo, RS; Joinville, S.C.

**Pastor Ray and Ruth Holter** served in Cruz Alta, RS; Rio Negro, PR.

**Pastor Robert and Ruth Kasperson** served in Cianorte and Londrina, PR. Sponsoring congregation: Victory, Minneapolis, MN.

**Pastor George and Helen Knapp** served in Maringa, Londrina, and Campo Mourão, PR; and Vilhena, Rondonia. They were supported by the Evangelical Lutheran Church, United Missionary Church and Association of Lutheran Free Congregations.

**Pastor Elden O. and Lila M. Landvik** served in Presidente Prudente, SP and Taquara, RS. Sponsoring congregations: Vinje, Willmar, and Our Savior's, Virginia, MN.

**Pastor Robert C. and Ann M. Maland** served in Marília, SP; Caxias do Sul, Farroupilha and Bento Gonçalves, RS. Sponsoring congregations: Our Savior's, Perth Amboy, NJ; Bethany, Windom, MN; Zion, Rake, IA; Pontoppidan, Fargo, ND

**Pastor Fayette and Jeanne Massingill** served in Paranavaí and Rio Negro, PR.

**Pastor Peter E. and Elna M. Mathiasen** served in Loanda, Cianorte, and Ponta Grossa, PR. Sponsoring congregations: St. Mark's, Butler, PA; St. Paul's, Lynwood, CA; and St. Ansgar, Toronto, Canada.

Pastor Donald and Lorena Nelson served in Rosário do Sul, Pelotas, and Novo Hamburgo, RS; Campo Novo de Parecis, MT. Sponsoring congregations: Calvary, Park Rapids; Glyndon, Glyndon; Good Shepherd, Moorhead; First, Mahnomen; Immanuel, Clara City; Our Savior's, Canby; Our Redeemer's, Benson; Bygland, Fisher; Fisher, Fisher, all in Minnesota; St. Petri, Story City; Zion-St. John, Sheffield; Stratford, Stratford; Bethesda, Ames; Our Savior's, Radcliffe; Elvira-Zion, Clinton; and Elsborg, Pomery, all in Iowa; and Trinity, Loveland, CO; Faith, Albuquerque, NM.

Pastor Andy and Ardys Olsen served in Cianorte and Paranavaí, PR. Sponsoring congregations: New Hope and Hayti, Hayti, SD.

Pastor Gary and Karlene Peterson served in Paranavaí and Cascavel, PR; Taquara and Pedro Osório, RS.

Pastor James L. and Mary Jo Peterson served in Cianorte, PR; Vila Ema and Ferraz de Vasconcelos, SP. Sponsoring congregations: Grace, Eau Claire, WI; Zion, Pittsburgh, PA and Faith, Spicer, MN.

Viola Reed served in Cianorte, PR.

Pastor Robert and Alona Roiko served in Taquara, RS; Rio Negro, PR; Mafra, SC.

Pastor Odin Kenneth and Carola Stenberg served in São Paulo, SP; Juiz de Fora, MG; Londrina, PR.

Pastor Otto C. and Barbara J. Tollefson served in Cianorte, PR; Joinville, SC. Sponsoring congregations: Vangen, Mission Hill; Gayville, Gayville, SD; Shepherd of the Valley, Canoga Park, CA; Vining, Vining, MN; Ballard First, Seattle, WA; Salem, St. Paul, MN.

Pastor Richard and Dorothy Wangen served in Curitiba, PR; São Paulo, SP; São Leopoldo, RS. They were supported by the Lutheran World Federation. Sponsoring congregations: First Lutheran, Harvey, ND.